PMDD

Monthly Meltdown Manual

*Handling Hellish Hormones,
Havoc, Hysteria and Healing*

PUBLISHED BY: Sophie Barton

📕 Copyright Notice

© Sophie Barton, 2025. All rights reserved.

This book is protected under international copyright law. No part of this publication may be reproduced, stored in a retrieval system, or transmitted in any form or by any means, electronic, mechanical, photocopying, recording, or otherwise, without the prior written permission of the author, except for brief quotations used in a review or scholarly article.

This book is intended for informational and educational purposes only. It is not intended as a substitute for professional medical advice, diagnosis, or treatment. Always seek the advice of a qualified healthcare provider with any questions you may have regarding PMDD or any medical condition.

The recipes, lifestyle suggestions, and personal reflections shared in this book are based on the author's research, experience, and interpretation. The author makes no guarantees regarding outcomes or results.

All product names, brands, and other trademarks mentioned are the property of their respective owners and are used only for identification purposes. No affiliation or endorsement is implied.

Contents

Introduction 5

What on Earth is PMDD? 9

    The Hormonal Hell Loop: 10

    Why You Probably Haven't Heard of It 15

    The Many Faces of PMDD: 20

Life Before Diagnosis: 25

    The Gaslight Years: 26

    Diagnosis Roulette: 31

    The Calendar Clues: 34

    Doctor Roulette: 37

The Hormone-Sanity Connection: 45

    Hormonal Rollercoaster: 46

    Brain on Fire: 51

    PMS's Evil Twin: 54

Rage, Grief, and the Dark Side: 60

    The Rage That Scorches: 61

    Grieving Who You Thought You'd Be 64

    Intrusive Thoughts and the Edge of the Abyss 67

The Physical Symptoms 71

    Hormones Gone Wild: 72

    Pain in the Everywhere: 74

    Energy? Never Met Her: 77

Living With Someone Who Has PMDD 79

It's Not About You 80

The PMDD Survival Guide for Support Humans 85

Boundaries Are Sexy: 90

Surviving PMDD at Work and in Society that Expects You to Smile 94

The Mask and the Meeting: 95

Deadline Dread and Hormonal Havoc: 98

Smiling is Not a Coping Strategy: 101

Your Personal PMDD Toolkit: 104

Pick Your Potions: 105

Trusting Yourself More Than the Labels 111

Mood Maps & Cycle Hacks: 114

PMDD & Relationships: 125

Loving Me, Loving You: 126

Breakups, Boundaries & The Blame Game 131

Parenting with PMDD 134

The Guilt Spiral 135

Battle Planning 139

Help Is Not a Weakness 142

You Are Not Your PMDD: 147

Reclaiming Me: 148

Joy Isn't Cancelled: 151

Stronger Together: 154

Introduction

I can't pinpoint the exact moment I knew something wasn't right. I've always known my time of the month was extremely melodramatic when I compared my experience to others, but I guess I had always shrugged it off, assuming that this is just me for two weeks in every six, and I had to roll with the hormonal punches.

If you've opened this book, chances are that your hormones have gone wildly off-script. Maybe you're here to find out what's going on with someone you care about and want to learn how to actually *help*. Wondering how to best equip yourself with the right things to say and do. Whatever brought you here, you're not on this journey alone, and my hope is that this book becomes your toolkit and your much-needed lifeline.

Let me be blunt: PMDD is a beast.

In the simplest terms, it's a hormonal horror show.

I remember (on one too many occasions) being sat at my desk ready to take on the day, caffeine in hand. A minor setback happened, and I felt the PMDD monster within me rage. If it had a face, it would definitely be full-on, ugly crying, its chest heaving with devastation, as if it had just witnessed a tragic love story unfold before it's very eyes. Likely the cause was spilled milk, hypothetically speaking.

A day later, I'd be livid because my partner dared to breathe too loudly near me, shortly after having the cheek to fast forward a little too fast, and I had missed the opening line of the Traitors Round Table Final. This sent me into a full-blown rage spiral. And then, like clockwork, two days later "poof!", I was fine. As if none of it had happened. No more rage, no more despair, no more minor inconvenience-related trauma. Once again, I was left standing in the aftermath, utterly confused, feeling like my brain had been possessed by a very dramatic and slightly unhinged alter ego.

Sound familiar?

For years, I searched for answers. I blamed stress patterns, diet, the moon cycles, literally anything I could think of, before finally discovering that my monthly descent into madness had a name: premenstrual dysphoric disorder, or PMDD. And let me tell you, finding that name was both a relief and a slap in the face. Relief, because finally, I wasn't just too sensitive or overly emotional. I refer to it as a slap in the face, because when I tried to find a book to help me, all I could find were vague, clinical explanations or self-help guides that made it sound like a bit of yoga and positive thinking would solve everything. Spoiler alert: it didn't!

PMDD doesn't just crash into *you*, it unfortunately splashes onto everyone in the blast radius. Your partner, kids, best friend, and the poor barista who asked the *wrong* question at the *wrong* time, they all get caught in the emotional fallout. One minute you're laughing at cat memes, the next you're sobbing because someone left a dish in the sink "in a way that felt personal." It's not that we want to be dramatic, we're *hostages* to hostile hormones! But seriously, the guilt of snapping at a loved one or cancelling (again) because you're emotionally gutted is real. PMDD turns you into someone even *you* don't recognize, and watching it affect the people we care about is its own kind of heartbreak. It's like your brain gets hijacked, and your relationships get caught in the turbulence. And yet, somehow, they still love us. Saints, all of them. Tired saints.

That's why I wanted to write this book. Because PMDD is real, and it's hellish. It's not just bad PMS or being a bit moody. It's a full-body, full-brain assault that hijacks your emotions, your relationships, your productivity, and even your sense of self. One week, you're a functioning adult. The next, you're trapped in a hormonal tornado, feeling like an absolute monster until it all vanishes, leaving you dazed, confused, and often apologizing to everyone in sight. It can even do the utter opposite, making you emotionally numb, I'm not sure which is worse.

Sometimes, PMDD doesn't show up as a raging storm, it arrives like a heavy fog. You don't cry, you don't scream… you just *don't feel much of anything at all*. It's like someone hit the mute button on your emotions, and now everything's dulled out in grayscale. Joy? Meh. Motivation? Gone. That show you usually love? Feels like static. You know you *should* care, about work, people, life, but it's like your brain is running on low battery mode and all the feelings apps are closed. It's isolating, confusing, and weirdly exhausting to feel so flat. And the worst part? You *remember* what it's like to feel connected and alive, it's just locked behind some hormonal forcefield that refuses to budge. Your period then arrives, and the beast that hijacked your brain and body retreats until next month, when it will return like some cruel subscription service you never signed up for.

This is not a book that will tell you to just meditate your PMDD away or eat more leafy greens and try gratitude journaling (although, if that helps, fantastic, please do it). This is a book that acknowledges the real experience of PMDD, the rage, the tears, the exhaustion, the self-doubt, the sudden existential crises and says: Yep. This is awful. But we can make this manageable together.

Throughout this book, we're going to dive deep into the chaos of PMDD. We'll explore the science behind it, the emotional havoc it wreaks, and the ways we can claw back some control. There will be practical advice, real stories, and a little humour. Because if we don't laugh about this (at least a little), we might just cry and then rage and then cry again.

If you've ever found yourself apologizing for things you did or said right before your period, if you've ever felt like a stranger in your own mind, if you've ever had a meltdown over something completely ridiculous (and knew it was ridiculous but couldn't stop yourself), this book is for you.

Grab some snacks.

We've got a lot to talk about.

Chapter One

What on Earth is PMDD?

(And Why No One Talks About It)

The Hormonal Hell Loop:

PMDD vs. "Just PMS"

Let's get one thing straight, PMDD is not "just PMS with extra sass.". Sure, both happen in the two weeks before a period, but PMDD and PMS are about as similar as a paper cut and open-heart surgery.

One is mildly annoying.

The other can eat your brain alive, chew your self-worth, and set fire to your emotional equilibrium, all before you've even finished brushing your teeth. Said other also has a degree in emotional sabotage and a black belt in chaos

So, what actually *is* PMDD? In the simplest, no-BS way I can put it: Premenstrual Dysphoric Disorder is a severe, chronic condition where your brain goes temporarily off the rails in response to hormonal fluctuations. More specifically, it's a mood disorder tied to your menstrual cycle. You're not broken. Your brain just reacts to the hormonal shifts of your cycle, especially after ovulation, like someone threw a Molotov cocktail into your neurotransmitters.

During your menstrual cycle, hormones like estrogen and progesterone rise and fall. For most people, this is just part of the monthly grind. But for those with PMDD, something about this hormonal rollercoaster sends their brain into chaos mode. Scientists believe it's not about the *levels* of hormones themselves, but your body's *sensitivity* to them, kind of like how some people can eat peanuts and be fine, while others go into anaphylactic shock. Your brain is basically allergic to your own hormones.

Cue the luteal phase, the two-ish weeks after ovulation and before your period begins. This is when PMDD likes to barge in, uninvited, wearing clown shoes and swinging a wrecking ball through your life. One day you're fine, the next you're sobbing in your car over a pigeon that looked lonely. Or maybe you're rage-texting your partner because they forgot to take the bins out. Or you're completely numb, staring at the ceiling like your soul wandered off without leaving a forwarding address.

This isn't moodiness.

This is full-body emotional whiplash.

And yet, despite the soul-crushing intensity of it all, PMDD is still wildly misunderstood. You say "I have PMDD" and people blink like you said you're allergic to gravity. So, then you try "it's like really bad PMS," because that's what we've all been taught to say, even though the comparison is deeply, insultingly inadequate. PMS might make you cranky, crave chocolate, and cry at dog commercials. PMDD can make you question your worth, your relationships, and your will to keep going. It can make you feel like a completely different person, a person you don't recognize and sometimes don't even like. And then, like magic, your period starts… and poof. You're back. Like nothing happened. Except everything did.

Living with PMDD is like being possessed on a schedule. There's the "you" that functions, goes to work, texts friends back, eats vegetables, and then there's Luteal You, who might spend three hours obsessing over whether everyone secretly hates you, and another three curled up under a blanket trying not to exist. And this cycle repeats.

Month after month. Often for years.

It's like Groundhog Day, but instead of a cute rodents and mild life lessons, you get hormonal sabotage and emotional freefall.

Let me give you a few snapshots of what PMDD can actually *feel* like. Maybe you've lived this. Maybe you've Googled it at 2 a.m. wondering if you're going crazy. You're not. You're not even close.

It can feel like your brain is auditioning for a horror movie, but you're the director, the villain, and the victim all at once. You're filled with irrational guilt. You become convinced you're a burden to everyone around you. You can't stop picking fights with your loved ones, even as you watch yourself doing it in slow motion, screaming internally to stop, please stop, but you don't. The rage is real, and so is the despair.

Sometimes, PMDD is quiet.

It tiptoes in like fog and smothers your energy, motivation, and interest in life. You forget what joy feels like. You cancel plans. You stare at your phone, unable to reply. You feel blank, but underneath the blankness is a storm of shame. "Why can't I just pull it together?" you wonder, not knowing that it's not about strength. It's chemistry. It's biology. And it's not your fault.

Then your period arrives, and the clouds lift. Maybe not instantly, but noticeably. You start to breathe again. Laugh again. You scroll back through your texts or journal or mental mess and think, "What the hell just happened?" That's the Hormonal Hell Loop. And it's as real as any other chronic health condition, just sneakier, and far too often dismissed.

The worst part? Most of us spend years not even knowing PMDD exists. We're told it's stress. Depression. Anxiety. BPD. Just being "emotional." We try yoga, cut out dairy, download meditation apps, and blame ourselves when nothing works. Meanwhile, doctors shrug or prescribe birth control like it's a one-size-fits-all solution.

Spoiler: it's not.

For some, hormonal treatments help. For others, they make things worse. There is no magic fix. Just trial and error, and a whole lot of self-advocacy.

Talking about PMDD still feels taboo. Like people are uncomfortable hearing that your period doesn't just give you cramps, it makes you question your entire existence. But silence only fuels the shame spiral. So we have to speak up. We have to name it, curse it, laugh at it, write about it, and most of all, let others know they're not alone.

Because PMDD thrives in the dark. It feeds off isolation and invisibility. But when we drag it into the light, even just a little, it loses some of its power. And in that space, there's room for understanding. For community. For healing.

So, if you've ever found yourself googling "why do I hate everyone before my period?" or crying because your brain is holding you hostage every month, this chapter is your mirror. PMDD is real. It's brutal. And no, you're not being dramatic. You're being human, in a body that reacts intensely to very real biochemical changes.

The Hormonal Hell Loop is not your fault, and you're not stuck in it alone.

Welcome to the conversation we *should* have been having all along.

Why You Probably Haven't Heard of It
(Even if It's Been Wrecking Your Life for Years)

There's something deeply disturbing about living through what feels like an emotional demolition derby every month and still wondering, "Is this just me?" It's not. But if you feel like you're the only one Googling *"why do I lose my mind before my period?"* while crying into your cereal at 3 a.m., congratulations, you've stumbled into the beautiful, enraging mystery that is PMDD: Premenstrual Dysphoric Disorder.

If you've never heard of it until recently (or until right now), you're not alone. Most of us find out about PMDD the same way: not from a doctor, not from a health class, not even from that one very well-meaning friend who loves crystals and moon charts. No. We find out from a late-night Reddit post written by someone who sounds exactly like us, or a tearful TikTok that nails the invisible war inside our heads, or that one blog post where a stranger says, "I thought I was broken, but turns out it was PMDD," and you sob in relief because *same*.

So why haven't we heard of it?

Why is something that affects roughly **1 in 20 menstruating people** still so wildly under the radar?

Let me introduce you to an old friend: **medical gaslighting**. You know the drill. You show up to your GP with a full emotional crime scene in your brain, and they tell you it's probably just stress. Or you try to explain how you become a completely different person for part of every month, and they squint and suggest maybe it's anxiety. Or depression. Or BPD. Or "just hormones." Translation: they don't know, and instead of saying *that*, they imply it's all in your head. (It *is* in your head, but not in the way they mean.)

It's not entirely their fault. Most doctors get shockingly little training in menstrual-related disorders. Ask a medical student how much time is spent on PMDD in school and they'll say something between "none" and "blink and you missed it." It's like our reproductive systems are treated as optional side quests in the main story of human health. And unless you're lucky enough to find a doctor who specializes in hormonal health (and who actually listens to you), chances are you'll be bounced around the healthcare system like an unwanted group text.

Now layer in the centuries-old legacy of society downplaying women's health, especially anything to do with hormones. PMS jokes? Everywhere. "Must be her time of the month"? A classic workplace zinger. "Hysterical woman" trope? Alive and well in both fiction and real life. We've been trained to treat mood changes related to menstruation as a punchline, not a legitimate medical concern.

And if you do finally gather the courage to speak up, to tell someone that you feel completely derailed before your period, that your mental health nosedives like clockwork, that sometimes you don't even recognize yourself, you get one of three responses:

1. A blank stare.
2. "Yeah, I get moody too."
3. "Have you tried essential oils?"

When formal healthcare fails, I found that it's the informal spaces pick up the slack. It's in the comment sections, the private Facebook groups, the late-night forum threads where people piece together their experiences like amateur detectives. You start to realize your symptoms match theirs. You're not alone. You're not dramatic. You're just living in a body with a condition no one bothered to tell you about.

The first time I saw someone describe PMDD as "temporary monthly madness," I felt *seen*. And not in the polite, Pinterest-y way, in the gut-punch, "holy hell, someone finally said it out loud" way. Because when you're living it, it's more than mood swings. It's more than being "a bit hormonal." It's full-blown identity theft, where your own brain kidnaps you and leaves a doppelgänger behind who rage-cries, ghost-texts, and contemplates quitting everything and moving to a cabin in the woods. And then your period starts, and just like that, you're back. Like it never happened. Except it *did*, and you carry the fallout.

But because no one talks about it openly, we end up suffering in silence. We assume we're broken. We try to "fix" ourselves. Therapy helps, sure, but when your serotonin levels nosedive every 25-30 days due to a biological trigger, no amount of positive affirmations are going to rewire your brain chemistry.

(Shoutout to the therapist who finally said to me, "This sounds hormonal, not just cognitive." I could've kissed her.)

The invisibility of PMDD isn't just frustrating, it's dangerous. People have lost jobs, relationships, and years of their lives without ever realizing there was a name for what they were going through. Some end up in crisis. Some get misdiagnosed and medicated for conditions they don't have. And some, too many, are told it's all in their heads until they start believing it.

It doesn't help that PMDD doesn't show up neatly on a blood test. There's no single scan or marker that screams, "Here it is!" Diagnosis usually involves charting symptoms across multiple cycles and ruling out other conditions. It's more like a slow, frustrating game of hormonal Clue, where half the doctors haven't even read the rulebook.

And yet, somehow, we're expected to carry on. Show up to work. Parent our kids. Smile at the checkout line. All while secretly wondering why we can't "just snap out of it." The guilt is brutal. The shame is worse. And the silence? Deafening.

But here's the thing: once you *do* hear about PMDD, everything starts to make sense. You look back at years of chaos and finally see a pattern. You realize you're not weak or unstable or attention-seeking, you're navigating a condition that's been under-recognized for far too long. And that realization? It's a lifeline.

So yes, you probably haven't heard of PMDD until now. But now that you have, you can't un-know it. You'll see it in yourself, in your friends, in that colleague who disappears for a week every month and comes back exhausted but won't say why. You'll start connecting the dots. And maybe, just maybe, you'll feel a little less alone in this weird, wild hormonal circus.

Let's keep talking. Let's shout it from the rooftops or whisper it through DMs, whatever it takes. Because PMDD isn't rare. It's just rarely recognized. And that needs to change.

Preferably yesterday.

The Many Faces of PMDD:
It's Not One-Size-Fits-All

If you've met one person with PMDD, you've met... exactly one person with PMDD.

This condition doesn't come with a tidy user manual or a checklist that fits everyone. PMDD is more like a chaotic shape-shifter that morphs from month to month, person to person, brain to brain. It doesn't follow the rules. It doesn't wear the same face twice. And if you're looking for a clean, universal symptom list, you'll end up screaming into a pillow, or worse, gaslighting yourself because you don't "tick all the boxes." So let's just throw out the idea of a textbook experience right now. PMDD is *not* one-size-fits-all.

For some people, PMDD feels like emotional destruction, mood swings that hit like a wrecking ball, rage that scorches everything in a five-mile radius, or sadness so deep it makes gravity feel personal. For others, it's more physical: exhaustion that makes walking to the fridge feel Olympic, joint pain, bloating, brain fog so thick you can't remember how to spell your own name, and an overwhelming need to disappear into a blanket cave. And then there's the cognitive side, the intrusive thoughts, the spiralling doubt, the weird disconnection from reality, like you're watching your life through a warped filter.

One person might rage-clean their house at 1 a.m. and cry because the dish sponge is too yellow. Another might go numb, turn off their phone, and feel like the world is a little too loud to bear. Someone else might feel it in their bones, literally. Aching limbs, stomach cramps, migraines that laugh in the face of painkillers. And here's the kicker: all of these people *have* PMDD. None of them are "wrong." They're just living different versions of the same hormonal horror story.

This is where PMDD gets really tricky: because it wears so many masks, it often hides in plain sight. You might think, "Well, I'm not *angry*, I just shut down and dissociate, so maybe this isn't PMDD?" Or, "I don't get sad, I just become hyper-sensitive to noise and start irrationally planning a move to the mountains." Surprise: still PMDD. The emotional spectrum ranges from despair to irritability to flat-out chaos. The physical side can range from migraines to nausea to feeling like your skeleton might be trying to escape your body. And the mental effects? Let's just say losing your train of thought mid-sentence becomes a full-time job.

Even within one person, PMDD can shift and twist over time. What wrecked you last month might barely register next cycle. What was once tearful might become irritable. What used to be a foggy brain might turn into laser-focused overthinking and obsessive guilt. It's a moving target. And that's what makes living with it, and diagnosing it, so maddening.

Then, add layers. Because PMDD doesn't exist in a vacuum. It shows up inside real people with full histories, identities, and brains that don't always match the "default" medical model.

Let's talk neurodivergence for a second. If you're someone with ADHD or autism, chances are you're already living in a brain that processes the world a little differently. Now toss in a hormone sensitivity that messes with emotional regulation, sensory processing, sleep, and executive function. Fun, right? PMDD can amplify what's already hard, and if you're neurodivergent, your PMDD might not look like anyone else's. You might not even recognize the mood swings as "mood swings" because your baseline is already nonlinear. You might feel like your whole brain short-circuits and the world just *stops making sense*. And then, poof, it passes. You're back. Until next time.

Trauma history? Same deal. If you've lived through trauma, your body and brain already have a finely tuned threat radar. Add PMDD into the mix, and your reactions may feel more intense, more volatile, or more self-protective than others'. Your luteal phase might unearth buried feelings, flashbacks, or fears that feel like they come out of nowhere. And because trauma doesn't always announce itself politely, this intersection is rarely talked about, but it matters.

Then there's culture, which adds a whole other layer of silence and stigma. In some cultures, menstruation itself is taboo, let alone mental health. Admitting that your period brings on suicidal thoughts, rage, or paralyzing anxiety? Unthinkable. For many people,

PMDD gets buried under decades of "just be strong," "don't complain," or "you're being too emotional." And because there's often no language for PMDD in traditional or cultural frameworks, people suffer in silence, thinking they're weak or cursed or simply "not handling life well."

This is why visibility matters so much. PMDD isn't a "type" of person, it's a condition that shows up in people of every race, gender, body type, and background. It doesn't discriminate. But the world around us often does. That's why some people get diagnosed within a year, and others spend a decade getting misdiagnosed with depression, anxiety, or "life stress."

There's also the invisible labour of managing it. The spreadsheets. The mood trackers. The journaling. The attempts at luteal-phase meal prep and vitamin rituals and scheduling important conversations only in the follicular phase when you're "sane." The people with PMDD often become highly attuned to their cycles, not because they're obsessive, but because *they have to be*. If you don't track it, it steamrolls you. And even when you do, it still might. That's the cruel joke.

Here's the empowering truth buried under all this chaos: just because your PMDD doesn't look like someone else's doesn't mean it's less real. You don't have to fit the stereotype of "weepy woman screaming into a pillow" to count. You don't have to have *every* symptom to seek help. You don't have to apologize for only experiencing *some* symptoms and not others. Your experience is valid, even if it's not dramatic. It's still PMDD even if your life looks high functioning from the outside. You can hold down a job and still feel like you're dying inside. That counts.

PMDD is messy and complex and wildly inconsistent. You are living through something intense and under-recognized, and you are doing the best you can inside a system that often hasn't caught up.

So, whether your PMDD feels like a screaming banshee, a foggy ghost, a sad narrator, or a quiet saboteur, it's real. It counts. And so do you.

Chapter Two

Life Before Diagnosis:

A Mystery Wrapped in Mood Swings

The Gaslight Years:
"Is It Just Me?"

Before my diagnosis, PMDD felt like a haunted house I lived in full-time, only everyone else insists it's just a bit draughty. You swear the walls are breathing, the floorboards scream, and something unhinged is rattling inside the pipes (spoiler: it's you).

There's no flashing neon sign over your head that says, "WARNING: HORMONAL HELL APPROACHING"

But time and again, you're told it's normal. Just hormones. Just stress. Just life.

Maybe a well-meaning friend has suggested, "Have you tried yoga?" (Which, to be clear, is lovely and all, but no amount of downward dog is going to wrestle PMDD into submission.)

For many of us, the road to understanding PMDD starts not with clarity, but confusion. The symptoms sneak in quietly, shape-shifting each month. You probably google things like "why do I hate everyone before my period" at 2 a.m., whispering your search terms like you're confessing to a crime.

The answers that come back?

"Take a bubble bath."

"Try journaling."

"Have you tried yoga?"

(Have you tried not being on fire, Karen?)

Let's rewrite the narrative that if we're struggling emotionally, it must be because we're weak. That if we're in pain, we should just push through it.

It's not just the world gaslighting you, it's yourself. When you hear "you're overreacting" enough times, you start to believe it. Maybe it *is* you. Maybe you *are* crazy. You start to edit your feelings in real time, second-guessing every emotional reaction like a movie script that needs toning down for mass audiences. You become a master of smiling through meltdowns and apologizing for things you don't understand.

If you've ever felt dismissed, ignored, or belittled for your symptoms, know this: It's not because you're exaggerating. It's because the world is still catching up to what you already know.

Take Cassie, for example. She recalls being told for years that she was "bad at coping." Her relationships faltered, her confidence tanked, and yet every time she tried to explain the depths of her despair, she was met with a soft chuckle and a "you're just hormonal, babe." She started scheduling breakups, breakdowns, and self-loathing spirals like clockwork, only she didn't realize there *was* a clock at all.

Then there's Jenna, who spent four years on antidepressants that did absolutely nothing for her cycle-related implosions. "I would tell my doctor, 'Hey, I'm only suicidal for about five days a month, does that mean anything?' and she'd just up my dosage. I started to feel like I was making it up, like I must be the problem because the medication wasn't fixing me."

That's the cruellest part of The Gaslight Years. The narrative isn't just that you're wrong, it's that your very perception of yourself is flawed. Your instincts become suspicious. Your emotions are recast as overreactions. You don't trust your own mind, and that is an incredibly lonely place to be.

Even our coping strategies, in hindsight, are part-tragic, part-comedic. A woman, Naomi, told me she used to prepare "emotional survival kits" she'd hide around her house: a bag of sour candy and tissues in the sock drawer, a self-written "you're not a monster" letter taped to the inside of the kitchen cupboard. "It sounds kind of crazy now," she laughs, "but at the time, it was pure desperation. I was white knuckling my way through half my life without knowing why."

And that's what it feels like. Half of your life, sometimes more, spent in a fog of misunderstood misery, questioning whether your reactions are real or if you're just fundamentally unwell. It's an exhausting, isolating, and often hilarious-in-retrospect period of life that many of us never even knew had a name until years later.

Eventually, a sliver of awareness cuts through the fog. Maybe you start noticing a pattern. Maybe a podcast episode, a stray article, or a desperate Reddit rabbit hole delivers the first whisper of PMDD. Suddenly, the last ten years of emotional whiplash begin to make sense.

In this chapter, we honour those gaslit years. We speak them aloud. Because if you've ever sat in your car wondering why your entire nervous system feels like it's short-circuiting, if you've ever questioned your own sanity because you couldn't stop crying over a minor inconvenience, if you've ever been called dramatic, needy, or too much, it was never *just you*.

It was always real. You were just too unhinged for the wrong people to understand. And now? You're starting to write a new story.

Diagnosis Roulette:
When Labels Don't Fit

Before PMDD entered the chat, many of us had already collected a small museum of misdiagnoses. Anxiety. Depression. Generalized anxiety *with depressive features*. Seasonal Affective Disorder. Borderline Personality Disorder. And, for the unlucky but extra "spicy," Bipolar II.

It starts innocently enough. You go to a doctor, therapist, or nurse practitioner with a trembling voice and tear-streaked cheeks. You say something vague but desperate like, *"I don't feel right."* And because you're articulate and trying so hard to "be good" at therapy, someone nods thoughtfully and gently hands you a label.

At first, it's a relief. A name. A reason. A starting point. But as the months, or years, go on, the puzzle pieces don't quite fit. The meds kind of help… until they don't. The therapy makes sense… except when it doesn't. You're still cycling, still swinging wildly between hope and hopelessness, rage and guilt, clarity and total detachment.

And so, the diagnoses change. Sometimes because you switch providers. Sometimes because the current label feels flimsy under the weight of your very real, very chaotic symptoms. Sometimes just because nobody can explain why you feel like you're dying for five days out of the month and then fine again by Wednesday.

Callie remembers being diagnosed with dysthymia in her twenties—"low-grade depression that's always there." But her depression wasn't *always* there. It was punctual, like a deeply toxic roommate who only moved in during the luteal phase. Still, she took her meds. She kept the journal. She did CBT. "I thought I was broken," she says. "The depression would just vanish some weeks. It made me feel like a fraud, even though I was clearly struggling."

Then there's Layla, who cycled through three therapists and two SSRIs before one doctor gently floated the possibility of Bipolar II. "It was like a punch," she recalls. "I didn't feel manic, but I *did* have this explosive irritability, this up-down emotional whiplash. And when someone says the word 'bipolar,' and you're already full of self-doubt, you just... accept it."

She wore the diagnosis like an ill-fitting jacket for years, tight in all the wrong places, sleeves dragging behind her, but it was the only thing she had to explain the noise in her brain. She joined support groups, tried mood stabilizers, and constantly wondered why none of it felt quite right. "I wasn't getting better," she says. "I was just getting quieter about it."

That's the thing about Diagnosis Roulette. You spin the wheel, and whatever label it lands on becomes your new reality, until it doesn't. Each misdiagnosis chips away at your confidence and adds another layer of grief: for the time lost, the self-trust eroded, the relationships strained by symptoms that were never properly understood.

There's power in hindsight. In finally finding PMDD and seeing the outline of yourself more clearly. The rage wasn't random. The despair wasn't just trauma. The cyclical nature wasn't a coincidence. It was always there, tucked inside your biology, screaming for recognition while the medical world reached for everything *but* the right answer.

Once you have the right label, when someone finally says, "Hey, I think this might be PMDD", there's a rush of relief and fury all at once. Relief because it makes *sense*. Fury because it took so damn long.

Reclaiming your story means rewriting all those years under the wrong diagnosis with a new lens. It doesn't erase the pain or restore the time, but it gives that pain context. And that's a kind of freedom.

You are not a failed treatment. You are not a diagnostic mystery. You are a person with a hormone-sensitive condition that's been neglected, overlooked, and under-researched for far too long.

The Calendar Clues:

Connecting the Dots

There comes a moment in many PMDD journeys that feels like both a revelation and a slap in the face. You're standing in the emotional wreckage of yet another meltdown, maybe you've just ugly-cried over a delayed Amazon parcel or dramatically declared you're moving to a forest to live alone with moss and regret, and then, it hits you.

Wait...

Isn't my period due?

Cue the mental montage: last month's existential crisis... the week before your period. That random argument where you told your partner they breathe like an entitled tit... also the week before. The crying-in-the-bathroom incident at work... you guessed it.

For the first time, you start lining up your emotional outbursts like little crime scene photos and realize, you're not unhinged, you're *cyclical*.

It's a strange relief, discovering you're not a complete mystery. You're a pattern. A hormonal murder mystery, maybe, but still a pattern.

Take Mel, who started tracking her cycle after a particularly dramatic week that ended with her sending an "I'm done with everything" group text to her family and then ghosting them for two days. "My sister gently asked me what day of my cycle I was on, and I rolled my eyes, but then I checked. I had PMS rage *on the same date* the month before. I felt like I'd cracked some secret code. I wasn't dramatic, I was data-driven."

Enter: the tracking apps. Suddenly you're downloading five at once, entering every symptom like a hormonal FBI profiler. "I cried at a lizard documentary." "Unreasonable rage toward dishwasher." "Spontaneous weeping while watching bread rise." And slowly, through colour-coded charts and terrifying graphs, the fog begins to lift.

You become your own forensic investigator, plotting mood swings on digital calendars and realizing that yes, in fact, you are possessed, but only between ovulation and menstruation. It's like solving a puzzle where the missing piece was *your entire hormonal system*.

Some people find this moment empowering. Others feel a deep rage at how long it took.

Both reactions are valid.

Alex describes her discovery like this: "When I saw the pattern, I felt both vindicated and furious. All those years I thought I was mentally unstable? Turns out I was hormonally betrayed on a schedule. I laughed, then I cried, then I made a colour-coded spreadsheet called 'Why I'm Not Actually Crazy.'"

Connecting the dots can bring a new kind of clarity. You begin to prepare for the PMDD phase like a storm chaser: snacks stocked, plans scaled back, supportive texts drafted in advance. Some people even give names to their PMDD selves, "Doom Week Me," "Hormonal Harriet," "Apocalypse Barbie", to separate the identity from the intensity.

It's not about trivializing the struggle. It's about reclaiming it. Giving yourself context, a heads-up, a way to say: *this isn't me being irrational, this is me navigating a chemical tidal wave with a leaky emotional raft.*

Once the pattern becomes visible, it doesn't solve everything. But it explains so much. And explanation is powerful. It makes room for compassion. For preparation. For choice. It means you're not reacting blindly anymore, you're responding with awareness.

If you've ever felt like your life was a chaotic sitcom directed by a hormonal trickster god, know this: once you start charting the madness, you get to write some of the script. You're not lost, you're just learning the map. And now that you've found it, the path forward gets a little clearer, one dot at a time.

Doctor Roulette:
The Trials and Tribulations of Being Taken Seriously

If there were a game show called *"What Fresh Hell is This?"*, I'd have been a regular contestant during my pre-diagnosis years. Picture me: dishevelled, mildly unhinged, clutching a symptom diary that looked like it belonged to a conspiracy theorist.

Cue flashing lights and the host shouting, *"Spin that Doctor Wheel!"*

Would I land on Dismissive Old White Guy?

The Patronizingly Calm Woman Who Writes "stress?" on a post-it?

Or my personal favourite, The Psychiatrist Who Thought I Needed to Forgive My Mother?

Reader, I hit them all.

The first time I brought up the pattern of my symptoms, I had been tracking them for six months in a little floral notebook like the type you'd use for wedding planning or gratitude journaling. It was filled with entries like, *"Day 21: shouted at barista, then cried because he didn't spell my name right. Day 22: contemplated quitting job, family, and possibly planet. Day 23: suicidal ideation, again. Period started Day 28. Feeling okay."*

I handed it to my GP, heart racing. She skimmed it, looked up, and said, *"Well, have you tried magnesium?"*

I stared. "Yes," I said. "And B6, and evening primrose oil, and meditating until I dissociated. I need help. Not Pinterest."

She told me it sounded like PMS and that I might benefit from cutting back on screen time. I wanted to cut back on existing. But sure, let's start with Instagram.

Another doctor suggested it was depression, even though I told him that I only felt like I wanted to crawl out of my skin during a very specific window of time every month.

He didn't even flinch. Just nodded and said, *"Well, maybe you're not noticing it the rest of the time."*

Oh, I notice. I notice every moment I'm *not* fighting the urge to cry because someone left crumbs on the kitchen bench. I notice when I can suddenly breathe again, like some hormonal fog has lifted, and I remember I don't actually hate everyone. Just sometimes. Very predictably.

When I finally got referred to a psychiatrist, I thought, *This is it. My redemption arc.* I sat down and told him everything, how the rage came in waves, how I'd become convinced once a month that I should leave my partner, quit my job, and start over somewhere remote and forested with no social interaction ever again.

He nodded and said, *"Sounds like unresolved family trauma."*

I blinked. "What?"

"I think if you made peace with your parents, some of this intensity would go away."

Now, to be fair, I do have unresolved family trauma, who doesn't? But my brain chemistry was clearly hijacking my life on a cycle that matched up *perfectly* with my hormones. I didn't need a family tree, I needed a hormonal map and probably a specialist, maybe a small exorcism.

It became a sick game. I'd walk into each appointment knowing I had to pitch myself in a very specific way: unhinged enough to be taken seriously, but not so unhinged that I was dismissed as dramatic or mentally unstable. There's a narrow window where women get believed, and let me tell you, it's as exhausting as it is humiliating to navigate.

One time, I tried a different approach. I went in completely prepared: charts, symptom trackers, articles, even screenshots from PMDD forums. The doctor barely glanced at them.

"You're working full time?" he asked.

"Yes," I said, "but barely holding it together. I spend half the month in a state of pure internal panic or despair."

I recall him looking at me (barely), almost looking through me. Bored? He's heard this one to many times. "Well, that's just being a woman". I couldn't believe it…

That comment sits in my soul like a forgotten tampon, deeply uncomfortable and quietly toxic. I wanted to scream, *Do you think we just get to opt out of life because we're suffering?* Women have built entire careers, raised families, and run governments while bleeding and breaking inside. We function *through* pain, not in the absence of it.

Still, I kept going. Because somewhere inside me, underneath the exhaustion and the self-doubt, was a woman who *knew* she wasn't crazy. I knew what I felt. I knew the timing was too precise to be random. I knew it was real, even when no one would name it.

Finally, finally, I found someone who listened. I walked into yet another GP's office, my usual stack of symptom trackers in hand, and instead of glazing over, she leaned in.

"You're describing PMDD," she said simply. "Let's look into it properly."

No magnesium. No lectures on my screen time. No gentle suggestion that I "relax more." Just recognition. It felt like someone had lifted a brick off my chest.

I cried in the car after that appointment. Not the messy kind, the quiet, steady kind that happens when you've been holding your breath for too long and someone finally gives you permission to exhale.

Getting that diagnosis didn't solve everything. But it gave me a narrative. A way to talk about it. A way to begin demanding better care, better support, better understanding, from others and from myself.

I still get angry about the years I spent feeling like a basket case because I was given the wrong labels. I still shudder at how casually suicidal thoughts were brushed aside. And I still wonder how many other women are out there, spinning the wheel, praying they land on a doctor who actually gives a damn.

If you're reading this and you're in that phase, maybe you're on your fifth doctor, maybe your fifteenth, don't give up. You're not "too emotional" or "not trying hard enough." You're in the middle of *Doctor Roulette*, and it sucks. But keep playing. Keep pushing. Keep walking out of those offices that don't serve you and into ones that might.

Because you deserve answers. You deserve care. And you deserve a life not dictated by a condition you didn't ask for.

The system may be broken, but we are not.

And we are far more resilient than they give us credit for.

How to Talk to Your Doctor About PMDD:

Scripts + Smart Prep

Navigating the medical system can be intimidating, especially when you're trying to explain something as complex and often invisible as PMDD. But being prepared can make all the difference.

☐ Opening Scripts: What to Say at Your Appointment

These are simple but clear ways to start the conversation:

Script 1:

"I've been tracking my symptoms and I think I may have Premenstrual Dysphoric Disorder. My mental and physical health changes drastically during certain parts of my cycle, and it's significantly affecting my life."

Script 2:

"Every month, about a week or two before my period, I experience severe symptoms, depression, rage, anxiety, that disappear once I start bleeding. I've read about PMDD, and I'd like to discuss whether that could be what I'm experiencing."

Script 3 (if the doctor is dismissive):

"I understand PMDD isn't always easy to diagnose, but I've come with data showing a clear cycle-related pattern. It's impacting my ability to function, and I'd appreciate an informed look into this."

☐ What to Bring: Your PMDD Symptom Data

Doctors love data, and when you come prepared, they're more likely to take you seriously. Here's what you can track and bring:

📅 Symptom Diary (2–3 cycles minimum)

Bring either a physical chart or app screenshots from tools like Me v PMDD, Clue, or Flo. You want to show:

- Dates of symptom onset and offset
- Severity of each symptom (0–10 scale works well)
- Specific symptoms (mood swings, irritability, fatigue, bloating, suicidal ideation, insomnia, etc.)
- The pattern, that they recur during the luteal phase and resolve with menstruation

📽 Example Table:

Date	Day of Cycle	Symptoms	Severity (0–10)
Jan 5	Day 21	Rage, crying spells, hopelessness	9
Jan 6–10	Day 22–26	Anxiety, body aches, extreme fatigue	8

Date	Day of Cycle	Symptoms	Severity (0–10)
Jan 11	Day 27	Period started, symptoms disappeared	2

📋 Additional Items:

- Family history of hormonal or mood disorders (if known)
- A written statement of how PMDD impacts work, relationships, or safety
- A list of all current medications, supplements, and previous diagnoses

☐ Extra Tips for the Appointment

- **Use medical language when possible** (e.g., "cyclical symptoms," "luteal phase," "suicidal ideation").
- **Ask directly**: "Are you familiar with PMDD and the DSM-5 diagnostic criteria?"
- **Bring someone supportive** if you fear being dismissed or overwhelmed.
- If dismissed, don't be afraid to say: "I'd like a second opinion" or seek a gynaecologist, reproductive psychiatrist, or hormone specialist.

Chapter Three

The Hormone-Sanity Connection:

Understanding What's Actually Going

Hormonal Rollercoaster:
Buckle Up for the Ride You Didn't Buy Tickets For

Welcome to the PMDD Theme Park, home of the world's most unpredictable thrill ride: *The Hormonal Rollercoaster*. Please secure your emotional support snacks, lower your expectations for stability, and keep your hands, feet, and sanity inside the vehicle at all times. You didn't ask to be here, but hey, at least we can learn how the ride works.

It all begins in the Follicular Forest, a deceptively peaceful part of the park. This is the calm before the chaos, the part of your cycle right after your period ends, where estrogen rises gently like the click-click-click of the rollercoaster car climbing up the first hill. You feel… dare we say… functional. Hopeful, even. Your brain is firing, your moods are stable, and you might even start reorganizing your sock drawer for fun. Estrogen is your trusty safety bar here, it keeps your brain supported, your serotonin flowing, and your optimism on track. You're upright. You're breathing. You're smiling at strangers.

Then, boom. You reach the Ovulation Summit, the peak. The view is incredible. Estrogen is at its highest, and progesterone starts to show up to the party. This is the moment in the cycle where you might feel invincible or at least semi-tolerant of group texts. If PMDD were purely about "hormones gone wild," we'd just be hormonal here too, but most people with PMDD actually feel okay during ovulation. That's important. Because what comes next? That's the plunge.

Cue the Luteal Loop. This is where the track drops out beneath you. Estrogen nosedives, serotonin decides to ghost you, and progesterone, who was *maybe* helpful in small doses, has now taken over the control booth with a megaphone and no chill. Imagine estrogen as your seatbelt and serotonin as the padding on the safety bar. When those vanish? You're just flying through the air hoping not to smack into a support beam. Progesterone becomes the upside-down loop-de-loop, and you're gripping the edges of reality wondering why you suddenly feel rage at the sound of someone chewing toast.

This is the part of the ride where your body, in a purely biological sense, is preparing for a possible pregnancy, even though your brain is preparing for a total emotional collapse. For those with PMDD, this shift isn't a gentle bend in the tracks. It's a full derailment. The communication between your hormones and your brain's neurotransmitters goes haywire, leading to symptoms that aren't just "moody" or "a little bloated." We're talking identity crises, rage spirals, existential dread, and panic attacks because someone looked at you weird. The difference isn't in the hormones themselves, we all go through the same cycle, but in *how our bodies react* to those changes. PMDD is about **sensitivity**. You're not broken. You're just wired differently.

Then finally, we roll into Menstruation Station, blood, cramps, maybe a little relief. The rollercoaster pulls into the dock. You're exhausted, dazed, mascara-streaked, and wondering how you didn't jump off halfway through. This is the reset button. The hormonal chaos begins to settle, the safety bar lowers again, and slowly, so slowly, your brain starts to feel like yours again.

And just when you think, *"Okay, that was awful but maybe it's over,"* the click-click-click of the climb starts again.

Here's what's important: this ride isn't your fault. You didn't design it, you didn't build the tracks, and you sure as hell didn't ask to board. But understanding how it works?

That's a kind of power.

Because when you know that estrogen and progesterone are the frenemies driving this deathtrap, when you know the exact part of the track where the plunge begins, you can start planning. Maybe even installing some metaphorical seatbelts of your own.

You're not weak for struggling here. You're a damn warrior for riding this thing every single month, and still getting up the next day. So keep your eyes open, keep learning the curves, and know that even when the ride feels endless, there *is* a return to solid ground.

You didn't buy tickets, but here you are. And you're doing better than you think.

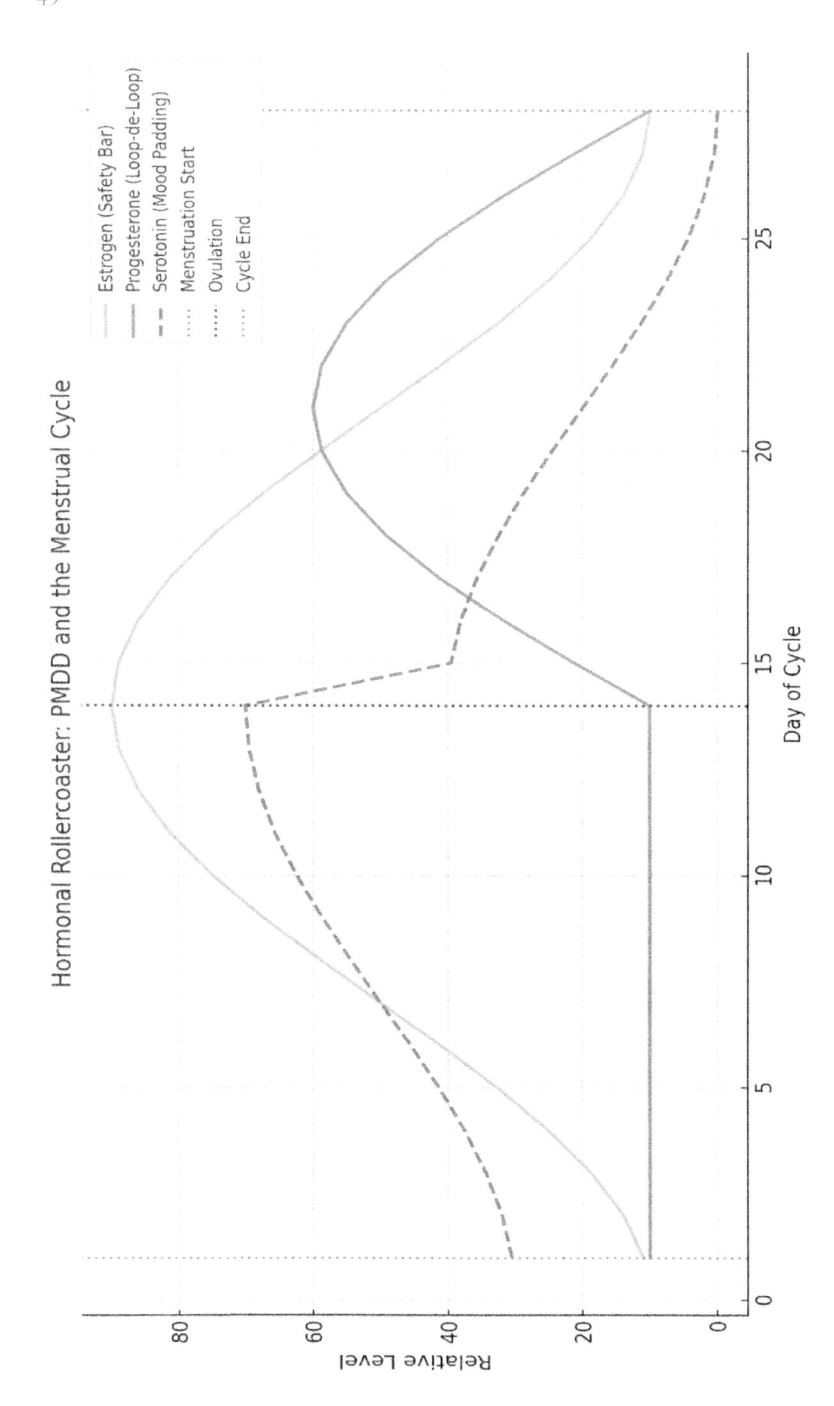

Hormonal Rollercoaster: PMDD and the Menstrual Cycle

— Estrogen (Safety Bar)
— Progesterone (Loop-de-Loop)
-- Serotonin (Mood Padding)
⋯ Menstruation Start
⋯ Ovulation
⋯ Cycle End

Here's a visual metaphor for the *Hormonal Rollercoaster* showing estrogen, progesterone, and serotonin across a typical 28-day cycle:

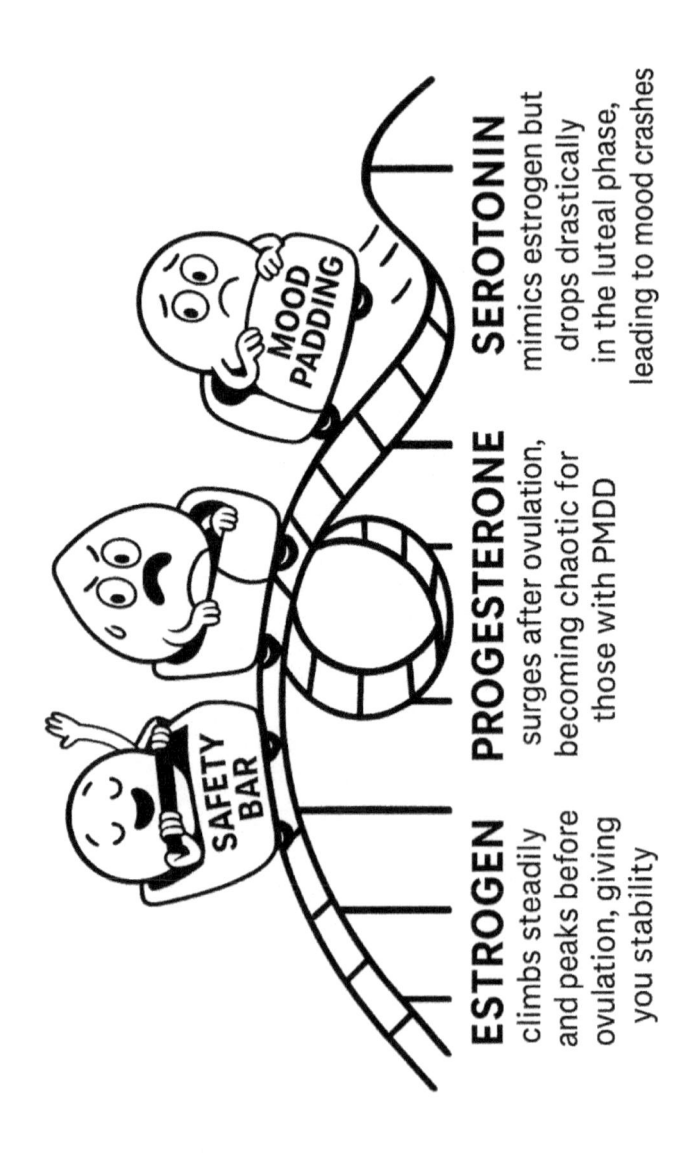

ESTROGEN — climbs steadily and peaks before ovulation, giving you stability

PROGESTERONE — surges after ovulation, becoming chaotic for those with PMDD

SEROTONIN — mimics estrogen but drops drastically in the luteal phase, leading to mood crashes

Brain on Fire:
Why You Can't Just "Think Positive"

Imagine your brain as a high-tech control room: glowing buttons, flickering monitors, little levers labelled "Mood," "Anxiety," "Sleep," and "Impulse Control." Normally, this room is managed by a team of competent, caffeinated neurotransmitters, serotonin, GABA, dopamine, calmly flipping switches and adjusting dials to keep you regulated and functional.

Now imagine it's the luteal phase of your cycle. Hormone sensitivity kicks in like a rogue raccoon in a NASA cockpit. Estrogen drops, progesterone rises, and suddenly those neurotransmitter interns are screaming, ducking under desks, and playing whack-a-mole with buttons that once kept you sane.

This is what it's like living with PMDD. It's not that you're *overreacting*. It's that the machinery has been hijacked.

Let's break it down. Estrogen, our trusty safety bar from the previous ride, doesn't just influence your body, it's a key player in brain chemistry too. It helps regulate serotonin, the "feel-good" neurotransmitter that makes you feel calm, stable, and able to tolerate the guy who clips his toenails at work. When estrogen crashes (as it does pre-period), serotonin takes a nosedive too. Less serotonin means more mood swings, irritability, sadness, and for many of us, a dark spiral into despair.

Then there's GABA, your brain's natural anti-anxiety chill pill. It keeps you from freaking out when you can't find your keys or when someone says "We need to talk." Progesterone, interestingly, interacts with GABA in a very "love me/hate me" kind of way. For some, it increases GABA's calming effects. But for people with PMDD? It can short-circuit the whole system, making you feel anxious, panicked, and like your skin is buzzing from the inside out.

And dopamine, the motivation molecule, also gets caught in the hormonal storm. That sense of joy when you finish a task or laugh at a meme? Gone. Replaced by emotional brain fog, executive dysfunction, and a heavy cloak of *why does everything feel so hard?*

The truth is, PMDD isn't a personality quirk or a lack of willpower. It's a **neuroendocrine disorder**, which means it lives at the messy intersection of hormones and brain chemistry. That makes it very real, very physical, and completely immune to well-meaning advice like "just go for a walk" or "have you tried journaling?"

Yes, sometimes journaling helps. So does movement, nutrition, therapy, meds, but none of those things are magical off-switches for a brain being ambushed by its own internal wiring. Telling someone with PMDD to "think positive" is like telling someone in a burning building to "just breathe." Helpful in theory. Useless when the fire alarm is blaring, and the ceiling is falling in.

What makes this even harder is that PMDD symptoms disappear when the period begins, which means for two-thirds of the month, you might feel "fine." This makes people question the bad days: *Was I faking it? Was I being dramatic?* No. You were experiencing a very real, temporary, but brutal malfunction in your brain's chemical communication system.

Next time it feels like your emotions are hijacking your entire sense of reality, pause. Take a breath. Remind yourself: *This is neurological.*

It's not your fault.

It's not your identity.

It's not forever.

The control room might be in chaos now, but help exists. You can learn where the fire extinguishers are. You can train new staff. Your brain is just dealing with a wildly unpredictable power surge.

You're doing the best you can inside a system that's short-circuiting.

That's not weakness.

That's survival.

PMDD – Month Madness Manual

The Medical History of PMDD

Ah, the rich, dusty halls of medical history, a place where women's mood swings were once blamed on wandering wombs, full moons, and general female "fragility." Yes, before we had the language (and science) to name Premenstrual Dysphoric Disorder (PMDD), we had centuries of eyebrow-raising theories, patriarchal finger-pointing, and some truly wild guesses. Buckle up—we're about to take a tour through time and see how we got from ancient superstition to modern science.

Wombs on the Move: *Ancient Theories and the Birth of "Hysteria"*

Long before we had hormones and neurotransmitters in the medical vocabulary, ancient Greek physicians had a different explanation for women's mysterious emotional outbursts: the uterus had gone rogue. Hippocrates, the so-called "Father of Medicine", believed that the uterus could literally *wander* around a woman's body, wreaking havoc as it went. Chest pain? The womb was pressing against your lungs. Dizziness? Clearly the uterus had ventured into your head. Feeling irritable or sad? Must be womb-induced melancholy.

This charming diagnosis was called "hysteria," from the Greek word *hystera*, meaning uterus. That's right, our entire emotional state was blamed on a temperamental reproductive organ staging a monthly protest march across the body.

Treatment options ranged from marriage (obviously) to forced intercourse (yikes) to aromatic therapies meant to lure the womb back into place. No one thought to ask women what they were actually feeling, or why.

Medieval Melodrama: From Hysteria to Witchcraft

Fast-forward to the Middle Ages, and things got darker (and weirder). Now, women's mood changes weren't just inconvenient, they were *dangerous*. Emotional volatility, particularly around menstruation, was seen as a potential sign of demonic possession. PMS? No, no. Possession by evil spirits. Logical.

Women who expressed rage, sadness, or other "unladylike" behaviours could be diagnosed not with a medical condition, but with being witches. Many were punished, isolated, or worse. The womb had taken a backseat, and now it was your soul that was under suspicion.

Needless to say, treatment was less about healing and more about control. Sound medical advice was replaced with exorcisms, prayers, and sometimes literal trials by fire.

Enlightenment Era: Sanity and Science (Sort Of)

By the 18th and 19th centuries, medicine began dipping its toes into the idea that maybe, *just maybe*, women's mental health issues were not spiritual curses or rogue uteruses, but something physiological. Still, the diagnosis of "hysteria" stuck around like an unwanted houseguest. Doctors of this time often described women as "nervous" or "high-strung," and prescribed rest, sedatives, or the infamous "rest cure" (which involved complete isolation and a lot of bed rest).

Meanwhile, men experiencing depression or anxiety were labelled with more neutral, respectable diagnoses like "melancholia" or "neurasthenia." The gender bias in medicine was as thick as molasses in January.

Still, some physicians began recording patterns, particularly the recurring nature of mood symptoms linked to menstruation. But without the tools to measure hormone levels or observe brain chemistry, everything stayed anecdotal. It was like trying to solve a jigsaw puzzle blindfolded, with half the pieces missing.

The 20th Century: From PMS to PMDD

With the rise of psychoanalysis in the early 20th century, mood-related menstrual symptoms took on a new interpretation. Freud, ever the drama king of psychology, attributed many women's issues to "repressed desires" and childhood experiences. Once again, hormones were not the focus. If you were weepy or enraged right before your period, it was probably because you wanted a baby. Or didn't want a baby. Or hated your mother. Or were just being a typical woman. Thanks for the clarity, Sigmund.

Then came the 1950s and '60s, a time of cocktails, cigarette ads for "housewives," and the emergence of a new term: **PMS** (premenstrual syndrome). This was progress! Sort of. PMS acknowledged that the menstrual cycle could affect mood and behaviour. However, it was still often dismissed as a punchline. PMS became shorthand for "woman being difficult," and not a legitimate medical concern.

The more severe experience, what we now recognize as PMDD, was often lumped into this general "monthly madness" category. If you had suicidal thoughts, debilitating rage, crushing sadness, and felt like an entirely different person for half the month? Well, take a Midol and get over it.

The DSM Milestones: PMDD Gets Its Name

Real change began in the late 20th century, as researchers started taking the hormonal-brain interaction seriously. In the 1980s and '90s, studies began documenting the severity of symptoms in a subset of people with PMS, people who weren't just irritable, but *incapacitated*. Emotional dysregulation, anxiety, depression, and impaired function, these symptoms didn't fade into the background. They took centre stage.

In 1994, the **DSM-IV** (that's the Diagnostic and Statistical Manual of Mental Disorders, fourth edition) included PMDD, but only in the appendix, under "criteria sets for further study." Translation: "We see you. We just don't *quite* believe you yet."

Finally, in 2013, with the release of the **DSM-5**, PMDD was officially recognized as a distinct psychiatric condition. This was a massive win, not just symbolically, but practically.

It meant real diagnostic criteria.

It meant validation.

It meant that women (and AFAB individuals) dealing with PMDD could access treatment options, insurance coverage, and most importantly, medical legitimacy.

Chapter Four

Rage, Grief, and the Dark Side:

What No One Tells You

The Rage That Scorches:
When You Don't Recognize Yourself

There is a kind of rage that doesn't simmer. It detonates. One minute you're folding laundry, and the next, you're fantasizing about launching a basket of clean socks out the window because your partner left a single dish in the sink again. It's not a cute, sassy anger. It's a tidal wave. It's "scorched earth" in yoga pants.

If you're nodding in uncomfortable recognition, welcome to the rage side of PMDD.

This rage feels like it comes out of nowhere. It doesn't build gradually or politely announce itself. It arrives like a bear crashing through your living room, flipping the couch and roaring in your face. The worst part? Sometimes *you* are the bear. And you watch it happen, helpless and horrified, from somewhere deep behind your own eyes.

Let's talk about one of those moments, you know the ones. Like when you're driving, and someone cuts you off, and suddenly you're not just annoyed, you're visualizing pulling over and giving them an entire TED Talk on driving etiquette, possibly while crying. Or the time you snapped at someone you love with a venom you didn't even know you were capable of. Later, you're flooded with shame, replaying the scene like a crime documentary. Who *was* that?

This is the unspoken horror of PMDD rage. It's not just being angry, it's feeling possessed by an emotion so loud and overwhelming that it drowns out everything else. Logic? Gone. Compassion? MIA. The version of yourself you usually know and like? Hiding under the bed with a bag of snacks and a blanket.

And then, when the storm passes, you're left in its wake, raw, remorseful, and confused. There's this horrible shame hangover. You apologize. You explain. Sometimes you cry. Sometimes you don't even have the energy to feel anything anymore. And in all of this, there's a gnawing fear: "Am I actually just… a terrible person?"

PMDD rage is not a character flaw. It's not your true self "coming out." It's a physiological storm, a neurological and hormonal upheaval that scrambles your internal chemistry until your emotional reactions are no longer proportional, fair, or even recognizable.

Your brain goes into DEFCON 1, and you're just along for the ride, white-knuckling the wheel and trying not to crash into everyone emotionally.

Still, I get it. It's hard to separate yourself from your symptoms when they show up wearing your face, using your voice, and torching your relationships. And society isn't great at giving women space to be angry in the first place, let alone *this* angry. So, it's easy to feel like you're the problem. That you're dramatic. Or unstable. Or dangerous. But the truth is, your emotional system is on fire, and you're doing your best not to burn the house down.

What's often missing in conversations about PMDD, and rage in general, is compassion. Not just from others, but from ourselves. We need to stop asking, "Why can't I control this?" and start asking, "What am I up against here?" You're up against a condition that floods your brain with intensity and then leaves you to clean up the mess. That takes guts. That takes strength. That takes grace, even when you don't feel graceful at all.

Rage doesn't have to be forever. There are treatments, coping strategies, medical options, lifestyle shifts. But before you can address any of that, you need to know one thing: *you are not a monster*. The rage isn't your truth, it's your brain on fire. And the fact that you feel shame afterward? That means you care. That means your core self is still very much intact, even if she sometimes gets buried under hormonal rubble.

If you're reading this after a bad day, a hard week, or a month that felt like one long scream, I see you. You're not alone in the rage. And you are still worthy of love, respect, and peace, even when you're struggling to find it inside yourself.

This chapter isn't here to fix you. It's here to hold your hand in the fire and say *I know. I know how hot it gets. And I also know that it will pass.*

You are not the storm. You're the one surviving it.

Grieving Who You Thought You'd Be

PMDD doesn't just take a sledgehammer to your mood. Sometimes, it quietly chips away at your sense of self. Not all at once. Not in a way that's easy to explain at brunch or in a therapy session. But over time, you start to realize there are parts of the person you thought you'd be, hoped you'd be, that just... never got to exist.

And grieving that? That's real.

Maybe you imagined yourself as someone who could handle a high-powered job, three kids, and a social calendar with colour-coded tabs. Maybe you saw yourself as the laid-back friend, the fun parent, the calm partner. Or the person who'd wake up early, go to yoga, and spend the day writing novels in a sun-drenched café without crying over the barista putting oat milk instead of almond.

But instead, you're here, navigating a disorder that can make getting out of bed feel like an Olympic event. You track your cycle like a secret codebreaker. You cancel plans because you can feel the switch flipping. You've had to explain, over and over again, that "I'm not myself this week" isn't an excuse, it's a warning flare. And you've probably lost people along the way. Friends who didn't get it. Jobs that didn't flex. Dreams that didn't survive the monthly demolition.

And even if you're resilient, even if you've built a life with scaffolding and support and sheer determination, the grief still lingers. Because somewhere in all this, you've had to let go of who you thought you'd be when life was easier, when your brain was calmer, when your body wasn't your biggest obstacle.

Here's what no one tells you: that grief is legitimate. It deserves space. You don't have to only feel grateful for what you *can* still do. You're allowed to feel sad for what PMDD has taken, not forever, not as your whole identity, but in real, human moments of reflection.

This grief isn't dramatic. It's not self-pity. It's the quiet heartbreak of realizing you're living with a different rulebook than most people. That some months feel stolen. That there are dreams on hold, or shelved entirely, not because you didn't try hard enough, but because your hormones turn you into a stranger half the time.

People don't often talk about this. The conversation around PMDD usually stops at "mood swings" or "hard periods." But that doesn't touch the depth of it. The way it reshapes your goals. The way it demands that you reorganize your entire life around your cycle. That's not just inconvenient, that's identity-altering.

Let me tell you something else that's true: grieving doesn't mean giving up. It doesn't mean your best self can't still show up, even if she's had to take a few detours. You may not be the person you imagined, but that doesn't make you lesser. In fact, it might make you braver, wiser, more tuned in to the rhythm of your body and the reality of what it takes to show up anyway.

You've probably learned things most people never have to. How to listen closely to your inner world. How to rebuild yourself after each crash. How to advocate for your needs in a society that barely knows PMDD exists. And yeah, maybe your life doesn't look like the Pinterest board version of success, but maybe that's okay. Maybe you've forged a version of strength that doesn't look pretty, but damn, is it powerful.

If you're mourning something today, a job you had to quit, a friendship that couldn't weather the storm, a version of you that never got to unfold, let yourself. Light a candle. Cry in the shower. Stare at the ceiling and say, "That wasn't fair." Because it wasn't. And honouring that is not weakness. It's healing.

You are a person carrying a heavy load in a world that rarely makes room for it. And still, here you are.

Still dreaming. Still hoping. Still becoming.

Intrusive Thoughts and the Edge of the Abyss

Let's go there. The part no one wants to talk about. The part that makes even the bravest among us pause before saying it out loud, in case someone looks at us like we've just confessed something shameful instead of something human.

Intrusive thoughts. Suicidal ideation. The mental spiral where everything feels too heavy, too loud, too endless. Welcome to the shadowy edge of PMDD.

There is always a way back. This chapter is here for you, not to sugarcoat anything, but to sit in the dark with you and remind you that someone else has been there, too.

PMDD doesn't just give you mood swings. Sometimes it grabs the steering wheel and aims straight for the cliff. The thoughts don't feel like *your* thoughts. They're not logical. They're not reasonable. But they show up anyway, uninvited, like a bad guest who insults your living room and drinks all your emotional energy.

Maybe the thought sneaks in softly:

"What if I just... stopped existing?"

Maybe it's louder: "I can't do this anymore."

Maybe it's terrifyingly specific.

And then, almost immediately, the shame crashes in. "Why am I thinking that?" "What if I tell someone and they freak out?" "Am I dangerous?" "Am I crazy?" Spoiler alert: you're not. You're in pain. There's a difference.

Intrusive thoughts are a symptom. They are not the sum of who you are. Your brain, in PMDD mode, is like a malfunctioning fire alarm, it's screaming "DANGER!" even when nothing is burning. So it starts pulling up exit plans. Not because you actually want to die. But because your nervous system is so overwhelmed that it wants *out* of the current state of suffering. It's panic, not logic. It's exhaustion, not truth.

Here's the raw part: it's terrifying to admit. Because people don't always get it. PMDD is still a fringe acronym in the mental health world. Too many of us have gone to professionals who blinked blankly at us or reached for the "Have you tried yoga?" card while we were clinging to emotional survival.

Of course we learn to hide it. To pretend. To smile and show up and say we're "just tired." Meanwhile, we're holding our minds together with duct tape and coffee and the hope that next week, we'll feel human again.

But pretending is exhausting. And the silence? That's what really isolates us. So, let's shatter it, gently but firmly. You are not the only one who has thought the unspeakable. You are not the only one who has cried in a locked bathroom or stared into the void of the ceiling at 3 a.m. wondering how much longer you can keep doing this.

There's nothing shameful about needing support. In fact, it's heroic. You deserve to be taken seriously. You deserve a care team that understands that your mental health is not just "hormonal" in the dismissive sense, but *hormonal* in the clinical, biological, complex, real-as-hell sense. You deserve treatment plans, not platitudes.

And you deserve to know this: there is life beyond the abyss.

I know, in the depths, it doesn't feel possible. But it is. There are people living fully now, people who once stood exactly where you're standing, peering into that void and thinking, "I can't do another cycle like this." But they did. And then they got help. And then things started to change.

It doesn't always get better overnight. But it does get *different*. More manageable. Softer around the edges. There are medications, therapies, tools, strategies, and people who *get it*. You don't have to keep carrying this in silence.

If today is one of those days, if the thoughts are loud, if the darkness is thick, take a breath. Text someone. Message a hotline. Cry, scream, write angry poetry on your phone. Whatever keeps you tethered. You don't have to be okay right now. You just have to stay. Because even if you don't believe it yet, the world needs you. In all your messy, hurting, brave glory.

You are not your thoughts. You are not your darkest day. You are not alone. And you are *absolutely* not too much.

You're just a human, navigating a hurricane inside your head.

And you're still here.

And that, my friend, is strength.

Chapter Five

The Physical Symptoms

Not Just in Your Head (It's in Your Boobs, Back, and Bones Too)

Hormones Gone Wild:

The Body Betrayal

Pain is one of the most insidious aspects of PMDD. If it's not cramps that feel like your uterus is staging a rebellion, it's the joint pain, headaches, and general body soreness that can hit you like a tidal wave. You didn't ask for this; it just showed up on your doorstep uninvited.

There comes a point every month where you find yourself staring into the fridge, bloated like a balloon animal, nipples on high alert, and wondering why your entire skeleton seems to ache. Is it the flu? Did you sprain your uterus in your sleep? Nope, just your monthly hormonal apocalypse, also known as PMDD. Welcome to the body betrayal portion of the program.

Let's touch back around on hormones. Those tiny little chemical messengers with God complexes. One minute they're doing their job, keeping things ticking along nicely. The next, they've formed a mutiny and are torching the village. Estrogen drops, progesterone skyrockets, serotonin taps out, and cortisol struts in like it owns the place. The result? A body that feels like it's trying to expel you from itself.

Your skin is suddenly puffy and everything you own feels like it shrunk in the wash. Bloating becomes a sport, how much air *can* one abdomen hold before liftoff? You consider Googling "am I secretly a water balloon?" but decide against it because your fingers are too swollen to type. Then there's the boobs. Oh, the boobs. Tender doesn't even begin to cover it. It's more like, "if someone brushes past me in the supermarket, I might scream and sue."

And the fatigue? PMDD fatigue isn't just "I stayed up too late" tired. It's "I just woke up and already need a nap, a massage, and a week off life" tired. It's a soul-deep exhaustion that no amount of caffeine can fix. It shows up like an uninvited houseguest and settles in, stealing your energy, your will to tidy up, and sometimes your ability to form a coherent sentence. You start to wonder if your bones are tired too.

Then there's the clumsiness. Oh yes, PMDD loves to mess with your coordination. Suddenly you're bumping into door frames and dropping everything. Your body no longer seems entirely under your control. It's like your hormones are in the driver's seat, and you're just a slightly dazed passenger clutching a crumpled road map with no idea where you're headed.

This hormonal chaos is real. It's measurable. It's cyclical. It's science and suffering in equal measure. You deserve more than a dismissive "that's just PMS." This is PMDD, and it's a full-body experience that deserves to be taken seriously, even if we laugh about it to survive.

Because sometimes, humour is all we've got. That, and stretchy pants.

Pain in the Everywhere:
Cramps, Aches & the Mysterious Full-Body Misery

Let's just start with, it's not "just period pain." It's not "just stress." And no, you didn't "sleep funny." PMDD pain is the kind of discomfort that creeps into every nook and cranny of your body and sets up shop like it's paying rent. It's sneaky, relentless, and somehow always manages to show up right when you need to function like a human.

First, the cramps. Not your run-of-the-mill, hot-water-bottle-and-you're-good type. We're talking cramps so fierce, it's like your uterus is training for a WWE smackdown, against *you*. They radiate down your thighs, wrap around your lower back, and make sitting, standing, or existing feel like a tactical operation. Sometimes, they're dull and constant. Other times, they stab you out of nowhere like your insides have beef with you.

PMDD isn't content with one area, it's more of a full-body experience. Your back might seize up like it's trying to remind you of that one time you sneezed wrong in 2017. Your joints ache like you've aged thirty years overnight. Knees, wrists, fingers, nothing is safe. Even your neck and jaw might get in on the action, just to keep things interesting. You start to feel like a walking stress knot.

Let's not forget the migraines. Not just headaches, *migraines*. The kind that hijack your entire day, make light and sound feel like torture, and force you to consider whether gouging out your eyeballs would be less painful. (Not really, but yes, it gets that dramatic.)

This kind of physical discomfort can make you doubt yourself. It's often invisible, so people don't see it. And because it moves around and changes, it can feel hard to describe, or worse, easy to dismiss. You might even find yourself questioning your own pain. Am I imagining this? Is it really that bad? (Answer: yes, it is. And no, you're not imagining it.)

Medical gaslighting is real again in this instance. Being told "everyone gets cramps," or "maybe it's anxiety," when your entire body is screaming for relief is a special kind of invalidation. But you're not being dramatic, you're being *systemically ignored*. That's why naming it, writing it down, and advocating for yourself isn't complaining, it's survival.

So, if you're curled up with a heating pad, surrounded by painkillers, wondering why it hurts to exist, know this: you are not alone. Your pain is real, even if it moves, morphs, and doesn't come with a visible rash or bruise. And you deserve to be believed, by your doctors, by your friends, and most importantly, by yourself.

Invisible pain doesn't mean imaginary pain. And if your body is shouting, it's doing so for a reason. Listen to it. Trust it. Advocate for it.

Even if your uterus is a drama queen.

Energy? Never Met Her:
Fatigue, Insomnia & PMDD's Sleepy Chaos

There's tired, and then there's *PMDD tired*. It's the kind of tired that doesn't care how early you went to bed or how many times you hit snooze. It's a bone-deep, soul-dragging exhaustion that wraps around you like a weighted blanket full of bricks. And just to make it extra fun? Sometimes it comes hand-in-hand with insomnia. Because, you know, sleep is for people who *don't* have hormonal sabotage on the agenda.

One of PMDD's most underappreciated magic tricks is making you both deeply exhausted *and* completely unable to rest. You lie in bed, exhausted from simply existing, yet your brain is hosting a 3 a.m. rave. Thoughts race, your heart may even flutter with that sneaky PMDD anxiety, and your body, which has been dragging all day, suddenly decides it's time to perform an Olympic-level mental gymnastics routine. Spoiler alert: nobody wins a medal.

Then morning comes, and you feel like you've been hit by a truck full of existential dread. Everything feels harder. The simple act of brushing your teeth can feel like a Herculean task. You're not lazy, and you're not unmotivated, your body is literally wading through hormonal sludge. Concentration? Shot. Motivation? Gone. Will to engage with other humans? Check back next week.

And the guilt? Oh, it shows up uninvited. The world doesn't pause for PMDD, so the pressure to "push through" is real. But it's hard to explain to your boss, partner, or friend that no, you're not just tired, you're experiencing what feels like a monthly shutdown of your internal power grid. And no, eight hours of sleep won't fix it, but thank you for the suggestion.

This fatigue isn't in your head. It's biochemical. The hormone chaos of PMDD messes with neurotransmitters like serotonin and dopamine, the very things that help regulate sleep, mood, and energy. Your circadian rhythm gets messed with. Your stress response gets amped. Basically, your body is doing the most while giving you the absolute least.

So, let's get one thing straight: your exhaustion is valid. Your need for rest is not a character flaw. Wanting to lie down for the entire second half of the month doesn't make you lazy, it makes you a human dealing with a very real, very consuming condition.

Sometimes, the bravest thing you can do is nap unapologetically.

Chapter Six

Living With Someone Who Has PMDD

(Without Running for the Hills)

It's Not About You

(Except When It Kinda Is)

Living with someone who has PMDD is like loving a volcano. For most of the month, it's just a mountain, majestic, maybe a little moody, but nothing you can't handle with a cup of tea and a respectful distance. Then, seemingly overnight, boom: lava, ash, and screaming into the void because someone forgot to take the chicken out of the freezer.

If you're reading this as a partner, roommate, friend, or family member of someone with PMDD, *thank you*. You're showing up, trying to understand, and that's already heroic. It means you care enough to learn, not just react. But buckle up, because understanding PMDD means stepping into a world where logic occasionally takes a back seat and emotional landmines are real. And most importantly: it's not about you. Well, *mostly* not.

See, PMDD is not just "bad PMS." It's PMS's demon cousin who shows up uninvited, rearranges the furniture, and makes everyone question reality for about a week or more every cycle. It's rooted in real brain chemistry, the kind that turns everyday stress into catastrophic despair, gentle questions into perceived accusations, and misplaced socks into symbols of the collapse of civilization.

So, when your partner suddenly weeps because you said "calm down" or reacts as if your suggestion to "go for a walk" was a personal betrayal, it's not about the words themselves. It's about how her brain is interpreting them, through a filter of cortisol, confusion, and a firestorm of internal static. She knows it's irrational. She probably hates it more than you do. But in that moment, reason is wearing noise-cancelling headphones.

When You Feel Attacked (and You Probably Will)

I want to talk about the elephant in the room: it *feels* personal.

Of course it does.

The tone is sharp.

The words are harsh.

Sometimes they're even cruel. Your natural response might be to defend yourself, argue back, or emotionally retreat. And who could blame you?

The tricky part? What she needs most in those moments is not to be corrected or challenged. She needs to feel *safe*. Because beneath the anger is often fear, and under the irritability is usually shame. PMDD doesn't just come with mood swings, it brings a sledgehammer to self-worth. The emotional outbursts? They're often followed by gut-wrenching guilt and exhaustion.

When she lashes out because you said "What's for dinner?", try to pause. Breathe. Remember that this isn't actually about you being a monster. It's about her brain misfiring under the weight of an invisible hormonal storm. That doesn't mean you have to be a doormat, far from it. But it means learning to respond instead of react.

Try saying, "That sounded really hard. Do you want me to listen or give you space?" instead of "Whoa, you're overreacting." Because while you may be *technically* correct (and trust me, your logical brain will want to be), choosing compassion over correctness is how you get through this with less collateral damage.

Ego vs. Empathy (Spoiler: Empathy Wins)

Your ego is going to take a hit. You may hear things that feel like emotional sniper fire. You may feel blamed, unappreciated, or just plain confused. But remember, PMDD isn't a referendum on your relationship or your value as a human being. It's a mental health condition.

Yes, she loves you. No, she's not faking it. And yes, she knows she's hard to be around right now, she probably hates herself for it. The irony? While she's mid-meltdown thinking she's the worst partner/mother/friend/roommate ever, you might be sitting there wondering if she's possessed by an angry Victorian ghost.

This is the emotional paradox of PMDD: the person with it is often painfully aware of their impact but powerless in the moment to control it. That's where your empathy matters. Not performative empathy. Not "I-read-a-Reddit-thread-on-PMDD-once" empathy. But the kind that says, "I see you're hurting, and even though this is hard for me, I'm still here."

You don't have to fix it. You don't have to say the perfect thing. Sometimes just being a calm, grounded presence, especially when she's unravelling, is the most loving thing you can do. Think lighthouse, not tugboat. Let her crash and rage and come back to shore when she's ready. Your steady light is enough.

Self-Preservation Is Not Selfish

Being a human port in someone's hormonal hurricane can be draining. You are allowed to take care of yourself, too. Loving someone with PMDD does not mean signing up for emotional martyrdom.

It's okay to take breaks, set boundaries, and say, "I love you, but I need ten minutes of silence to reset." You can offer support without absorbing all the chaos. You can validate her feelings without invalidating your own. Emotional safety is a two-way street. Don't abandon yourself in the name of being "supportive."

If you ever feel like you're walking on eggshells all month long, something's off. PMDD is serious, but it doesn't excuse abuse. If it crosses into that territory, it's okay to say, "This isn't working." Support doesn't mean staying silent or suffering. It means being honest and compassionate, with *both* people in the relationship.

The Aftermath (AKA PMDD's Apology Tour)

One of the most surreal parts of PMDD is what happens after the storm. The person who screamed at you for breathing too loud may now be tearfully apologizing and wondering if you secretly hate her. The shame hangover is real, and it's brutal. Be gentle if you can. Say what hurt, but say it with kindness.

Living with someone who has PMDD is a unique kind of emotional intimacy. It tests you, grows you, and sometimes makes you question your sanity. But it also teaches you about unconditional support, about love that sits beside suffering, and about holding space for someone when they can't hold it for themselves.

And yes, sometimes it *is* about you. Your actions, your tone, your presence, they all matter. But most of the time? It's about a brain in distress, a body at war with itself, and a woman doing her best not to drown in it.

Hold her hand.

Hold your boundaries.

And hold on tight.

The mountain will settle again.

The PMDD Survival Guide for Support Humans

First of all, congratulations. You've been officially initiated into the highly exclusive, slightly terrifying, and weirdly beautiful world of Supporting Someone With PMDD. You didn't sign up for this exactly, but here you are, Googling things like "Is this normal?" and "How to survive emotional whiplash without crying in the pantry." Gold star for effort. You're already ahead of 90% of the population just by reading this.

Supporting someone with PMDD is not about rescuing them. It's not about fixing, solving, or telling them to "go for a jog." If that's what you were hoping, I suggest putting this book down and backing away slowly before someone throws a hot water bottle at your head. Loving someone with PMDD is not a rescue mission. It's more like being a human beanbag chair, soft, supportive, and just present when they need to collapse.

Rule #1: **Do not, under any circumstances, ask "Are you PMSing?"** This phrase is the emotional equivalent of tossing a lit match into a puddle of gasoline and then acting surprised when it explodes. Even if you're 99% sure it's the luteal phase, even if your partner just screamed at a tube of toothpaste, resist the urge to diagnose. Nothing spikes the rage-o-meter faster than being reduced to a stereotype mid-crisis. Instead, try literally anything else. Ask how they're feeling. Say you've noticed things seem tough right now. Whisper "chocolate?" like a prayer. Anything but the P-word.

Let's talk about communication, which during a PMDD episode can feel like trying to talk to someone through a tornado while juggling raw eggs. What worked last week may suddenly be wrong. Harmless questions like "What do you want for dinner?" become emotional landmines. And somehow your very existence is simultaneously too much and not enough. Welcome to the paradox. The key is learning how to speak *with* someone in PMDD mode, not *at* them.

Rule of thumb? Be simple, clear, and kind. This is not the time for sarcasm or passive-aggressive quips. Don't say "You're being dramatic" or "You're overreacting", even if it feels true in the moment. It's not helpful, and it won't win you any awards for emotional intelligence. Instead, try things like "I can see this is hard" or "I'm here, what do you need right now?" And if they say "I don't know," respect that. Sometimes the most supportive thing you can do is *shut up and stay nearby*.

Which brings us to the Fixer Phenomenon. Ah yes, the noble urge to swoop in with your toolbelt of logic and reason and patch everything up. Newsflash: PMDD is not a plumbing issue. You cannot tighten a few bolts and stop the emotional leaking. And trying to do so often makes things worse. It says, "I don't trust your process. I just want you to stop feeling this way." And while that may be true (it's okay, you're human), it's not helpful.

Instead of fixing, think *holding*. Not literally, unless they ask, but emotionally. Be a container for their messy feelings without trying to clean them up. Say, "I've got you." Say, "That sounds like a lot." Say, "You're allowed to feel exactly what you're feeling." No solutions, no strategies, just space. They will probably circle back to logic when the storm passes. Right now? They just need to know they're not too much.

Let's also talk practical support, because not all heroics wear capes. Sometimes they wear sweatpants and make tea.

You might think you need grand gestures or dramatic interventions, but often it's the tiny, boring things that help most. Have a soft blanket ready. Know their favourite comfort foods (and have at least one stashed where no one else eats it). Offer to make dinner, or better yet, *don't ask if they want help, just do the thing*. Decision fatigue is real and brutal when PMDD is in full swing. If you can lighten the load without turning it into a performance, do it.

Memes can also be medicine. Yes, seriously. Sending a stupid, absurd, or lovingly dumb meme at just the right moment can break through the fog like sunshine through hormonal cloud cover. It says, "I'm thinking of you" without pressuring a response. Bonus points if it involves cats screaming into the void or penguins falling over.

Also, *respect the bubble*. Sometimes the best support is a wide berth. If they say, "I need to be alone," don't interpret it as rejection. It's often about self-preservation, not you. Let them have their cave time.

Leave snacks at the entrance like a medieval offering and walk away. They will emerge when they're ready. If they say "Don't touch me," don't pout. Just say "Got it. I'm here when you want me." Your ego will want to be needed. Don't listen to your ego. Listen to their needs.

And if you're thinking, "But what about *me*?", good. You matter too. You are not a doormat or an emotional sponge. Supporting someone with PMDD is intense, and it's okay to get tired. It's okay to feel frustrated. It's okay to go outside and scream into the void for a minute. Just don't scream *at* them. Make space for yourself. Decompress. Ask for help. You don't have to be perfect. You just have to be compassionate and consistent.

The person you're supporting likely *knows* how much they're putting you through. They may not be able to express it mid-meltdown, but trust me, the guilt avalanche that comes after is no joke. Your kindness? It's noticed. Your patience? Heroic. Your ability to sit in the emotional blast radius without running? That is love, in its rawest, most resilient form.

So to all the support humans out there, thank you. For being soft places to land. For staying present when things get loud and weird. For learning the difference between helping and hovering. You may never get a parade, but you *will* be the reason someone feels safe enough to get through the worst week of their month.

You're not here to fix. You're here to *hold*. And that, my friend, is more than enough.

What TO Say:

"I know this is really hard for you. How can I help?"...A little validation goes a long way. Just acknowledging that they're struggling makes them feel less alone.

"I'm here for you. No judgment, no pressure." PMDD can make people feel like a burden. Reminding them that you love them and aren't keeping score can be incredibly comforting.

"Do you need space, or do you want company?"...Some days, they'll want to be wrapped in a blanket like a burrito while binge-watching TV. Other days, they might need a human buffer to keep them from spiralling. Giving them a choice helps them feel more in control.

"I love you, even when PMDD is trying to convince you otherwise." PMDD messes with self-esteem. It whispers nasty little lies that make them feel unlovable. A reminder that you see *them*, not just the hormonal storm, can mean the world.

Boundaries Are Sexy:

Yours, Mine, and the Mood Swing's

Boundaries. Not the flimsy kind that come with a nervous smile and a "Sorry, but…" No. I'm talking about the bold, beautiful, deeply respectful kind that say: "I love you. I respect myself. And I'm not going to let either of us get steamrolled by this hormonal hurricane."

In the messy emotional ecosystem of PMDD, boundaries are not barriers. They are lifelines. And guess what? They're sexy as hell. There is nothing more attractive than someone who knows where they end and another person begins. It's not cold. It's not mean. It's not "shutting people out." It's making space for sanity, safety, and, if we're lucky, survival.

When PMDD hits, the vibe in the house can go from serene to spiralling faster than you can say "progesterone." Words are sharper, patience is thinner, and suddenly the simple act of breathing in the same room as someone can feel like a provocation. In that chaos, boundaries are what keep you from combusting, or combusting *at* each other.

If you're the person *with* PMDD, boundaries help you protect the people you love *from* the parts of you that don't feel like…well, *you*. That reactive, irrational, overstimulated creature who yells because the Wi-Fi is slow? She needs space. She doesn't need to be punished or shamed, she just needs a clear perimeter and a no-fly zone. Having the awareness to say, "I'm not in a place to talk right now" or "Please don't try to problem-solve me" is not weakness. It's not pushing people away. It's self-advocacy. It's care in disguise.

And if you're the person *supporting* someone with PMDD, boundaries are your emotional seatbelt. They're how you stay safe and present without getting pulled into the undertow. You're allowed to say, "I love you, but I need five minutes in the other room." You're allowed to excuse yourself from an argument that's spiralling. You're allowed to protect your peace *without abandoning your person*.

It doesn't have to be dramatic. You don't need a PowerPoint presentation or a therapist standing by. It can be as simple as: "This feels like too much right now. I care about you, but I need to come back to this when we're both calmer." The key is tone and timing. Don't lob your boundary like a grenade. Offer it like a warm blanket. Boundaries aren't rejection. They're structure. And structure, especially in the PMDD tornado, is love in action.

PMDD can turn the most loving relationships into emotional obstacle courses. There will be days when everything feels fragile. When one wrong word can trigger a meltdown, or a simple sigh is misread as a declaration of war. That's why mutual boundaries are the goal. Not just "don't talk to me like that," but also "I won't unload on you when I know I'm spiralling." Not just "I need space," but also "I'll let you know when I'm coming back."

Boundaries aren't one-sided, they're an agreement. They're built on trust, not control. And when they're respected, something magical happens: people feel safe. That safety is what makes intimacy sustainable. Not just romantic intimacy, but the deeper kind—the kind that says, "I see you at your worst, and I still choose to stay close… but not so close I lose myself."

Now let's talk about guilt, because that sucker loves to sneak in when you start setting boundaries. Guilt will whisper things like "You're being selfish" or "They'll think you don't care" or "This isn't what love looks like." But guilt is a liar. It's not selfish to need space. It's not mean to say no. It's not unloving to ask someone not to yell at you during a hormonal rage spiral. In fact, that's exactly what love looks like when things get hard: honesty with compassion, distance without disconnection.

And no, you don't have to get it perfect. You'll mess up. You'll set a boundary too late. You'll cave on one you meant to keep. You'll snap when you meant to stay calm. That's okay. The beauty of boundaries is they're adjustable. They're not stone walls, they're garden fences. Move them, repair them, reinforce them as needed. Just don't forget they're there for a reason.

There's also something deliciously empowering about watching someone you love honour their own boundary. Have you ever seen someone mid-breakdown say, "I need 30 minutes to decompress before we talk"? That's hot. That's emotional maturity. That's someone showing up for themselves, and by extension, showing up for you. And if you can mirror that energy? If you can say, "I'm here, but I'm also here for myself"? Now we're talking about a relationship with roots. Not co-dependence. Not burnout. But balance.

So next time the mood swing rolls in and everything feels high-stakes and fragile, pause. Breathe. Remember: you are not powerless. You have tools. And boundaries? Those are the heavy-duty, top-shelf, sexiest tools of them all.

Respect yours.

Respect theirs.

And respect the fact that even mood swings need fences sometimes.

Chapter Seven

Surviving PMDD at Work and in Society that Expects You to Smile

The Mask and the Meeting:
Pretending You're Fine with a Fire in Your Brain

There's a special kind of hell reserved for having to act "professional" when your insides feel like they've been hijacked by a hormonal demon doing cartwheels through your frontal lobe. It's like trying to host a PowerPoint presentation while someone slowly pours syrup into your brain and your soul screams quietly in the background. But sure, smile, contribute, circle back, and "touch base." No big deal.

Living with PMDD in the workplace is often a performance. And not the good kind with costumes and curtain calls. It's the exhausting kind, the one-woman show where you're expected to smile, nod, sound coherent, and remember acronyms while you silently calculate how many more hours you have to endure before you can crawl into bed and dissolve.

So, how do you do it? How do you survive meetings when your brain is short-circuiting and your nervous system is throwing a tantrum? You build your mask, but not the kind that hides you. The kind that *protects* you. This isn't about pretending you're okay. It's about giving yourself just enough camouflage to get through the moment without collapse.

Start with a few pre-planned lines. These are your emotional scaffolding, something neutral, polite, and easy to repeat when your mind goes blank or ragey. Things like "Let me get back to you on that," or "I'll make a note and follow up." These are golden. You don't have to be dazzling; you just have to be present enough to survive the interaction. Think of it like social CPR.

When possible, minimize your airtime. You are not a bad employee or a weak person for keeping your camera off or staying on mute when your head is pounding, and your mood has plummeted into the Mariana Trench. Not everyone needs to know you've cried in the toilet three times before 10 a.m. Give yourself permission to say less. The world doesn't crumble when you take a step back.

Boundaries are the scaffolding of sanity. If your brain is fogged over with PMDD static and you're expected to give a polished presentation, you're allowed to ask for a reschedule, or at least suggest a time when your brain might be more likely to cooperate. I know, I know, the world doesn't always allow for cycle-friendly calendars. But sometimes, asking is enough. Sometimes, your future self will thank you for that 48-hour reprieve.

Let's touch on knowing when to power through and when to pull the emergency brake. This one's tricky. There will be moments where you have to grit your teeth and get it done, and you will. Because you're brilliant and tenacious and terrifyingly competent even when you're falling apart. But there are also moments where the bravest thing you can do is say: "I can't today." Not because you're flaky or dramatic or can't handle stress, but because your body and brain are screaming for mercy. Listening to that scream isn't weakness. It's wisdom.

Surviving PMDD at work is an act of rebellion. You are not "overly sensitive." You're a goddamn gladiator showing up to battle while bleeding invisibly. The system isn't built for you. But you show up anyway, with dark circles under your eyes, a script in your head, and fire in your chest. And if today's the day you need to bow out? That's brave too.

You're doing your absolute best with a brain that tries to sabotage you once a month like clockwork.

Wear the mask when you need to.

Take it off when it's safe.

And remember, you're allowed to take up space, even when you're hanging on by a hormonal thread.

Deadline Dread and Hormonal Havoc:
Managing Productivity When Your Brain is Melting

Let's just say it: trying to be productive during PMDD is like trying to write a dissertation during a hurricane, while also fighting off the emotional equivalent of a raccoon in your chest. You stare at your to-do list with the same energy one might reserve for deciphering ancient hieroglyphs. Everything feels too loud, too hard, and entirely pointless, but the deadline remains, smiling menacingly from your inbox.

This is not laziness. This is not poor time management.

So how do you *work*, or at least fake functionality, when your brain is a hormonal stew of despair, rage, and inexplicable thirst for pickles and solitude? The secret is not working harder. It's working *differently*. Sneakily. Like a productivity ninja who knows her luteal phase is about to turn her brain into mashed potatoes.

First: time-block like your sanity depends on it. (Because let's be honest, it kind of does.) If you've started tracking your cycle, whether through an app, a journal, or sheer vibes, you'll notice the patterns. There are golden days when your mind is sharp, your energy is decent, and you remember where you left your keys. That's your prime time. Front-load the heavy stuff there: the strategy work, the big thinking, the meetings that require brain cells. Then, as your body begins to whisper *"It's coming..."*, shift. Downsize your expectations, cut back where you can, and prepare to lower the bar like it's limbo night.

But what about the deadlines you can't move? The emails you must answer? The meetings that just won't disappear no matter how much you stare at them with passive-aggressive intent? This is where you build in grace. That means setting "fake" deadlines a day or two early, padding your time estimates, and assuming that during PMDD week, your productivity will shrink like a wool jumper in hot water. Build around it, not against it. You're not failing, you're forecasting.

When the fog rolls in and your energy evaporates, backup systems become your best friends. Future You will be wildly grateful for anything Past You left behind, a draft, a checklist, a template, a half-written email. Think of it as leaving breadcrumbs through the forest for the version of yourself who can't remember her own middle name. Prepping for PMDD is no different from keeping cold medicine in the cabinet or charging your phone before a storm. It's not pessimistic; it's smart.

Let's tackle the awkward beast: talking about flexibility without turning it into a full-blown medical confessional. You don't owe anyone your reproductive history. You are allowed to say, "My workload is more manageable with some flexibility around these dates," or "I typically schedule lighter tasks in the second half of the month, just a rhythm that works best for me." That's it. You don't have to mention the fact that your brain chemistry temporarily rebrands you as a swamp witch. You are a professional, not a hormonal apology.

Let's retire the shame, shall we? You are not lazy, unreliable, or dramatic. You are navigating a recurring neuroendocrine crisis while still answering emails and contributing to the group chat. That is Olympic-level multitasking. Flexible working shouldn't be a privilege; it should be the norm. But until the system catches up, advocate for yourself with the quiet confidence of someone who knows that rest is a productivity tool, not a reward for suffering.

You're doing the best you can with a brain that temporarily unplugs itself every few weeks. Grace, backups, and kindness to your future self, those are your survival tools. The world may expect linear progress, but your cycle has other plans. Work with it. Not against it.

Smiling is Not a Coping Strategy:
Surviving Public Spaces When You'd Rather Scream

If you've ever found yourself holding back tears in the frozen food aisle because someone *looked* at you funny, or fantasizing about yeeting your entire soul into the void during a crowded commute, you already know: PMDD + public life = emotional landmine.

There is something uniquely awful about having to exist *out there* when your insides are in full mutiny. The noise, the lights, the smells, the relentless existence of other humans, it's all too much. And yet, the world expects you to show up with a perky smile and a "can-do" attitude like you're starring in a toothpaste commercial, not silently battling a hormone-fuelled apocalypse.

A classic: the casual "cheer up!" or "you don't look sick!" comments that land like bricks to the gut. First of all, thank you, stranger, for evaluating my face like I'm on trial for Bad Vibes. Second, no, I will *not* cheer up. I'm doing everything in my power not to weep or scream or explode into interpretive dance just to express the depth of my existential dread. So no. I will not.

In these moments, preloaded scripts are a game-changer. You don't owe anyone an explanation, but it helps to have a go-to line that draws a line politely but firmly. Something like: "Just keeping to myself today, thanks," or "Not up for a chat right now, but I hope you have a good one." If someone pushes? Channel your inner exhausted queen and give them a blank, unbothered stare that says: "I dare you." Because truly, we're done performing. That energy is being used to keep our molecules from disbanding.

Then there's commuting, aka navigating a gauntlet of smells, sounds, and human elbows while holding it together with mental duct tape. If there's ever a time to fake a "neutral face," it's here. Your version might be resting tired face, gritted jaw, or intense headphones energy. Wear sunglasses. Hoodie up. Pretend you're in an indie film about an emotionally complex loner. Whatever gets you through the bus ride without stabbing someone with a reusable straw.

Micro-boundaries. They're the tiny invisible fences you set to keep your inner peace from getting bulldozed by chatty baristas or over-friendly acquaintances. You can build these with body language, short answers, or even something as simple as not making eye contact. It's not rude. It's survival. You're allowed to prioritize your own nervous system over someone else's need for a good-morning grin.

Some days you'll have the strength to engage, and that's great. Other days, you'll walk through the world like a haunted Victorian child in a trench coat, silently screaming inside, and that's valid too. You don't owe anyone joy. You're allowed to feel miserable, uncomfortable, overwhelmed, or just plain done. Smiling is not a cure. It's not a strategy. It's a reflex we've been conditioned into, and honestly, it's overrated.

If you're trudging through public spaces with rage bubbling under your skin and your soul hanging on by a thread, know this: you're not a mess. You're a marvel. You're surviving something invisible, cyclical, and brutal, while still paying for groceries, answering texts, and occasionally managing not to scream in someone's face.

That, my friend, is resilience.

No smile required.

Chapter Eight

Your Personal PMDD Toolkit:

Customizing Your Coping Plan

Pick Your Potions:
Meds, Herbs & Magic Beans

This chapter is not about telling you what to do or which pill is your personal holy grail. It's about laying out the options like a really weird brunch buffet, some things you might love, some things you'll want to spit out, and others you'll sample with cautious optimism. Because if there's one truth we can all agree on, it's this: PMDD is not one-size-fits-all. And neither is managing it.

The Pharmaceutical Toolbox (Or: Big Med Energy)

Let's talk meds. For some of us, pharmaceuticals are the heavy lifters of PMDD management. Selective serotonin reuptake inhibitors (SSRIs), like fluoxetine (Prozac), sertraline (Zoloft), and citalopram (Celexa), are often prescribed either daily or just during the luteal phase. Yep, you heard that right. Some people take them for two weeks out of the month like emotional birth control. And for a lot of people, it helps — mood swings soften, intrusive thoughts lessen, and the urge to rage-quit life every time someone breathes too loudly may just retreat into the background hum of manageable irritation.

My Flirtation with Fluoxetine

So, there I was, crumpled on the bathroom floor for the third time that week, convinced my life was crumbling, again, when my doctor gently suggested what so many PMDD warriors have heard before: *"Have you tried fluoxetine? Just during your luteal phase?"*

Ah yes, the "two-weeks-on, two-weeks-off" solution. A hormonal half-marathon. The idea is straightforward in theory: start taking it two weeks after your period begins, that's around ovulation, and then stop when your period arrives. Like pressing a little green chemical button to hold yourself together while your hormones launch their monthly demolition derby.

I was hopeful. Desperate, really. The idea of not having to take something *every day* felt appealing, a smaller commitment, less medication, less... I don't know, dependence? So, I tried it. Dutifully swallowed my happy little pill halfway through my cycle. And then, just as I started to *maybe* feel like a slightly more functional human being, it was time to come off it again.

Cue: the crash.

Turns out, my body does *not* like being ghosted by serotonin. The come-up? Rocky. The come-down? Hellish. It felt like I was dragging my nervous system through a hormonal mosh pit on a bi-weekly schedule. I'd get side effects on the way in, nausea, jaw tension, foggy thoughts, just in time for them to start easing off... and then bam, off the meds again and back into the storm. Mood swings. Brain zaps. A weird hollow feeling that no amount of carbs could fix. And then, right when I'd finally stabilize, the whole circus started again.

It was like speed dating your neurotransmitters and getting ghosted every time.

For some people, this method works beautifully, genuinely. They float into their luteal phase, chemically cushioned, and then gracefully slide back out with their sanity intact. But for me? It felt like emotional whiplash. My body didn't like the switch-flip. It wanted either all or nothing, not this half-hearted relationship with serotonin.

We forget the *charming* side effects of some meds. The sudden loss of libido, the nausea that made toast feel like a risk, the weird twitch in my eyelid that may or may not have been stress-related. The "Is this my personality or is this the pill?" spiral that kept me up at night. And oh, the sweating. No one warns you about the sweating.

Eventually, after a lot of internal bargaining (and a few very dramatic journal entries), I switched to a daily low dose instead of the luteal-only method. And that, surprise, surprise, felt way more stable. Like I was finally giving my nervous system a little consistency instead of yanking it around like a marionette. The fog lifted more gently. My outbursts became less "fire and brimstone" and more "mildly irritated librarian." A win, if you ask me.

I'm not here to trash fluoxetine. Honestly, it helped. But the timing matters, and so does the method. What's often presented as a "one size fits all" solution needs way more nuance. Because your body isn't a machine, and your brain chemistry doesn't always like being yanked on and off a chemical leash like a hormonal light switch.

So if the two-weeks-on, two-weeks-off thing hasn't worked for you? You're not a failure. You're not "resistant." You're just... human. And this isn't about pushing through. It's about finding a rhythm that doesn't make you feel like a malfunctioning science experiment.

If fluoxetine's on your radar (or already in your bathroom cabinet), know this: it's okay to try. It's okay to stop. It's okay to take it differently than what the doctor originally suggested. And it's more than okay to *listen to your own body* over someone else's protocol.

You're not weak for needing help. You're brave for figuring out what works. And if that includes daily meds, or no meds, or taking breaks, or never taking them again, you're still doing it right.

Now excuse me while I go drink water, eat something with actual nutrients, and continue becoming best friends with my serotonin.

I won't sugarcoat it. SSRIs aren't a magic fix for everyone. Some people feel emotionally blunted. Others feel like they've swapped PMDD for persistent nausea or a sex drive that ghosted them and never returned their texts. It's trial and error. And often, it's trial and *more* error before anything feels even close to stable.

Then there's hormonal birth control. The idea here is to suppress ovulation altogether and skip the whole hormonal rollercoaster that causes PMDD symptoms in the first place. In theory, genius. In reality? It's a mixed bag. Some folks find glorious relief, a smooth hormonal baseline, no ovulation, fewer mood crashes. Others find themselves spiralling even harder, like they've been thrown from the frying pan directly into the abyss. This is why "just go on the pill" can feel like both a hopeful suggestion and a cruel joke, depending on your hormonal temperament.

Then there's the nuclear option: GnRH agonists (read: medically induced menopause). These are usually reserved for severe, treatment-resistant cases and come with a long list of caveats, including bone density loss and the sudden need to learn what "bioidentical hormone replacement therapy" means. But for those on the brink, it's sometimes a game-changer.

The key takeaway here? Meds can help. Or they can suck. Or they can help and suck at the same time. It's okay if you're not sure which camp you fall into yet. You're allowed to explore. You're allowed to quit. You're allowed to try again.

The Natural Remedy Nook
(For the Green Witch in All of Us)

Okay, so maybe you're supplement-curious. Or maybe you've reached the point where you're eyeing your houseplants and wondering if any of them are secretly medicinal. Enter the world of herbs, minerals, and oils, sometimes helpful, sometimes hokey, and always surrounded by just enough anecdotal evidence to keep you Googling at 2 a.m.

Let's start with Vitex (aka chasteberry), the poster child of natural hormone balance. Some people swear this stuff regulated their cycles, smoothed their luteal phase, and even tamed their inner gremlin.

Others… got acne, bloating, and a healthy dose of "what the hell is this doing to me?" As always: bodies vary.

Then there's magnesium. Now *this* one gets more universal applause, it supports sleep, reduces bloating, calms nerves, and helps keep you from drop-kicking your microwave just because your toast burned. It's not a miracle cure, but think of it as background support. Like the best friend who shows up with snacks and doesn't talk too much.

CBD, the non-high sibling of THC, is another fan favourite. It's praised for calming anxiety, easing cramps, and generally softening the chaos. That said, the CBD market is the wild west. Some products are brilliant; others are overpriced nonsense in tiny glass bottles. Research, start small, and don't feel bad if it's not your thing.

There are also B vitamins, omega-3s, evening primrose oil, and turmeric. Some people track every milligram. Others pop whatever softgel is closest and hope for the best. The truth? Natural remedies can be *part* of the puzzle, not the whole picture. If they help, great. If they don't, you didn't fail. You just checked another box on your personal experiment form.

Trusting Yourself More Than the Labels

Here's the thing no doctor, wellness guru, or internet forum can tell you better than your own body: what's actually *working* for you. Just because something is "clinically proven" doesn't mean it works for *you*. Just because something is "natural" doesn't mean it's harmless. And just because you've been doing something for a while doesn't mean you're not allowed to change your mind.

Doctors can offer guidance, and if you find a good one, they're golden, but at the end of the day, only *you* live in your body. Only you know the difference between "this is a side effect I can live with" and "this is stealing the light from my eyes."

Give yourself permission to be curious. Be a scientist in your own life. Don't commit to anything just because it's what worked for someone else. Try, track, adjust. You're not being flaky; you're being *responsive*.

Which brings us to your interactive moment...

☑ Remedy Radar: Two-Cycle Tracker

Let's track some data, not the sterile kind your doctor might ask for, but the kind that helps *you* actually feel seen. Here's a framework to print, screenshot, doodle in your journal, or adapt however you want:

Week 1 (Follicular Phase)

Mood: _____

Energy: _____

Remedy taken: _____

Any side effects or changes?

_____

Week 2 (Ovulation)

Mood: _____

Energy: _____

Remedy taken: _____

Any side effects or changes?

_____

Week 3 (Luteal – PMDD time)

Mood: _____

Energy: _____

Remedy taken: _____

Any side effects or changes?

_____

Week 4 (Menstruation)

Mood: _____

Energy: _____

Remedy taken: _____

Any side effects or changes?

_____

Now rinse and repeat for a second cycle. What patterns show up? When did you feel like yourself? When did things get worse? When did you want to throw your supplements out the window and declare war on your uterus? Note it all. These observations are gold.

Whether you're a med-taker, a plant-milker, a supplement-sipper, or a little bit of everything, remember this: *you're not doing it wrong*. The path to managing PMDD isn't a straight line; it's a wobbly, weird, often frustrating spiral, but one that still moves forward. Keep going. You're allowed to experiment. You're allowed to demand more. And you're absolutely allowed to mix science, magic, and whatever else it takes to feel okay again.

Now go fill your metaphorical potion shelf with whatever you damn well please. You're the alchemist here.

Mood Maps & Cycle Hacks:
Making the Calendar Your BFF

Living with PMDD means you don't just ride the hormonal rollercoaster, you build the tracks, steer the train, and sometimes scream into the void as it derails. But what if, instead of resisting the rhythm of your body, you started working *with* it?

This chapter is all about turning your calendar from a passive box-ticking torture device into a power tool. Not in a rigid, colour-coded, "boss babe" productivity way, but in a way that helps you feel less like life is happening *to* you and more like you're co-authoring your days with your hormones. Mood maps, cycle hacks, and a little planning sorcery can make a huge difference when it comes to surviving and even *thriving* with PMDD.

You in? Great. Let's sync your soul with your cycle.

First, Let's Get Real About the Phases

You don't need a biology degree to track your cycle, but you do need a little basic intel. Your menstrual cycle has four main phases: menstrual, follicular, ovulation, and luteal. Think of them like seasons. Each one brings its own mood, energy, superpowers, and, for those of us with PMDD, potential landmines.

The luteal phase, the 7–14 days before your period, is where PMDD symptoms tend to throw the biggest tantrums. It's where anxiety spikes, your tolerance for loud chewing drops to zero, and suddenly everyone you love is unbearable. That's not you being broken. That's a hormonal brew stirring up some very real neurochemical chaos. The goal here is not to *fix* it, but to *see* it. Then plan accordingly.

The good news is: the other phases? They're pretty damn useful. Your follicular phase (after your period ends) often comes with a dose of energy, clarity, and social sparkle. Ovulation can bring confidence, libido, and all-around hot girl energy. And menstruation? Well, despite the cramps and chocolate cravings, it's also a time for letting go and starting fresh. There's power in knowing where you are in the cycle and how to lean into it, instead of pushing against the tide.

Mood Journals, Apps & Wild Tracking Experiments

Now, before you start shading in calendars or downloading every period app with pastel branding, hear this: tracking your cycle isn't about perfection. You do *not* need to become a hormonally enlightened guru overnight. You just need enough data to notice patterns.

Some people love mood journals, jotting down each day's general vibe, what they ate, how they slept, if their partner annoyed them or if they felt like buying a puppy at 2 a.m. These little notes can reveal trends you'd never spot otherwise. Did your existential dread always hit on Day 23? Do you always feel like quitting your job and moving to a lighthouse the week before your period? That's not random. That's a map.

Apps can help too. Clue, Flo, and Hormona are some of the more thoughtful ones (less pink glitter, more science), and many now offer PMDD-specific tracking options. Some let you track physical symptoms, emotional states, and even medication effects — all in one place. There's something deeply validating about seeing a graph confirm that yes, you do feel like a different person in Week 3, and no, you're not making it up.

If digital isn't your thing, go analog. Colour-code a paper planner. Create a secret symbol system. Turn your mood into emojis in the margin. Whatever feels intuitive, not overwhelming. The point isn't to get *all* the data, just enough to better understand *your* cycle.

Scheduling Like a PMDD-Pro

Once you've got a few cycles of info under your belt, you can start to plan like a hormonal ninja. This doesn't mean locking your life into an inflexible pattern or ghosting responsibilities every time you bleed. It means giving yourself the *option* to align your activities with your energy and mood, where possible. It's a form of self-respect.

For example, if you know your luteal phase is a time when social interactions feel like emotional spelunking, *maybe* don't book three networking events or host brunch with your passive-aggressive aunt that week. Push the heavy conversations, dentist appointments, or emotionally charged tasks into your follicular or ovulation phase when your bandwidth is bigger. Need to deep clean your entire apartment or pitch a bold idea at work? Try to line that up with your post-period rise or ovulation high. These aren't hard rules — just gentle nudges toward harmony.

Of course, life happens. Sometimes your period comes early, or you have to give a big presentation mid-meltdown. That's okay. This isn't about control. It's about stacking the odds in your favour *when you can*, and offering yourself compassion when you can't.

Design Your Dream Month

Alright, it's worksheet time, not the boring kind, promise. This is your invitation to dream up a month that flows with your natural rhythm. We're not pretending life is always predictable, but there's something empowering about trying.

Imagine a calendar spread in front of you. Let's play.

Week 1: Menstruation. What would make this week more restful? Can you block a quieter day? Order groceries instead of dragging your bloated body to the store? Let this week be about softness, slowness, and solitude where possible.

Week 2: Follicular phase. You're likely feeling more energized, motivated, and clear-headed. This is prime time for to-do lists, workouts that don't make you cry, and the stuff you "couldn't even" last week. Where can you channel this spark?

Week 3: Ovulation. You might feel bold, chatty, flirtatious, or just generally magnetic. Great time to meet new people, have a date night, or take on something big and brave. What feels exciting, or just possible, during this time?

Week 4: Luteal phase. Now's the time for boundaries, cozy routines, and lowered expectations. If your brain gets foggy or your patience vanishes, that's not failure, that's biology. Can you reschedule non-urgent tasks? Say no a little more often? Give yourself permission to cocoon?

Draw it out, scribble ideas, colour-code it, burn it under the moon, whatever feels good. This isn't about productivity. It's about designing a life that doesn't punish you for being cyclical.

You don't have to be perfectly in sync to benefit from cycle-based planning. Even the smallest adjustments, like not scheduling back-to-back meetings when you know you'll be feeling raw, can create space for peace. Over time, this practice builds self-trust. It reminds you that your mood swings aren't failures of character, but ripples in a larger rhythm.

Let your calendar be more than just a list of things to survive. Let it be a love letter to your future self. One that says, "I see you coming. I know what you'll need. I got you."

Snack Your Sanity:

Feeding the Feels Without Guilt

You shouldn't feel guilty for craving salt, sugar, or cheese-stuffed carbs when PMDD comes knocking. Your body isn't betraying you. Your appetite isn't a moral failure. And that voice in your head whispering that you "should've had a salad" instead of a snack cake? Yeah, she can sit this one out.

This chapter is about food, not in a clean-eating, kale-worshipping way, but in a real, human, I-just-ate-an-entire-bag-of-chips-and-still-feel-empty kind of way. Because for those of us living with PMDD, food often becomes more than fuel. It becomes comfort, control, rebellion, relief, sometimes all in one bite. And we need to talk about it without guilt, shame, or diet culture garbage trailing behind.

The Real Talk: Food, Mood & Hormones

Here's the not-so-secret secret: what you eat can mess with or support your mood. This isn't a scolding. It's biology. Blood sugar drops, nutrient deficiencies, and hormonal shifts can create the perfect storm for cravings, fatigue, irritability, and full-blown meltdowns. That doesn't mean you need to ban cupcakes or start dry-brushing your intestines. It just means a little awareness goes a long way.

For example, when your blood sugar crashes (often after eating something super refined and sugary on an empty stomach), your mood might do the same. Cue the tears, the snapping, the sudden existential crisis in the cereal aisle. But when you've got protein, fibre, and complex carbs on board, things tend to feel a little more stable. Not perfect, just *less unhinged*. And sometimes, that's all we're going for.

Magnesium-rich foods like dark chocolate, nuts, and leafy greens can actually help calm your nervous system. Omega-3s in salmon and flaxseeds have been linked to mood regulation. Even keeping up with hydration can mean fewer headaches and slightly less rage at the sound of your partner breathing.

None of this is magic. None of this "fixes" PMDD. But feeding your body like it deserves to feel okay, even on the days it doesn't, is a radical kind of self-care.

Emotional Eating Isn't the Enemy

If you've ever shame-eaten a sleeve of cookies at 10 p.m. and then cried about it while promising to start a "clean eating" plan tomorrow, you're not alone. Emotional eating is deeply human. We reach for food not because we're weak or undisciplined but because we're trying to *soothe* ourselves in a moment that feels impossible.

That's not failure. That's coping.

The trick is not to eliminate comfort eating, but to make peace with it and expand your toolkit. Maybe sometimes you want to cry-eat a grilled cheese sandwich while watching videos of baby goats. Do it. No apologies. And maybe other times you realize that what you're really hungry for is something warm, grounding, and actually satisfying, like roasted sweet potatoes, miso soup, or a good old-fashioned peanut butter banana situation.

What matters is that you're choosing with awareness, not punishment. There is no perfect food. There is no bad food. There is just you, doing your best not to scream at a tree or dissolve into sobs in the frozen food aisle. That deserves compassion, not calorie counting.

High-Energy Prep for Low-Energy Days

Now let's talk strategy, because while spontaneous snack fests can be glorious, having some pre-thought-out feel-good food options on hand can seriously reduce your luteal-week chaos. The key is to harness those "follicular-phase goddess" days (you know the ones, where you feel productive and full of potential) and use them to prep for the week when everything feels too hard, including chewing.

We're not talking about meal prepping in a Pinterest-mom way. No colour-coded containers or quinoa pyramids required. Just little, thoughtful things your future self will thank you for. Think: making a batch of soup, freezing a few burritos, chopping veggies, or having snack packs of almonds and dried fruit ready to go. Buy the emergency chocolate now. Put the kettle on for future-you. Think of it as love letters from the version of you who has her sh*t somewhat together.

Even prepping a "luteal phase drawer" in your pantry or fridge can help, stuff that's easy to eat, not too overwhelming, and doesn't make you feel worse after. Include comfort foods *and* nourishing ones. You're allowed to have both. This isn't about restriction. It's about support.

Stock your space with little things that make eating feel cozy and kind: your favourite mug, a ridiculous spoon, a candle that smells like you have your life together. Surrounding your meals with softness counts, too.

Cravings Are Not Crimes

Somewhere along the way, we were taught that craving food, especially as women, was shameful. That we're supposed to be dainty and disciplined and "above" our biological urges. But let me say this loudly for the people in the back: CRAVINGS ARE NOT CHARACTER FLAWS. They are messages from your body, your brain, or both, and they deserve to be heard, not punished.

Sometimes a craving is your body asking for something, salt, carbs, fat, warmth, pleasure. Sometimes it's your emotions screaming for a sense of control or comfort. Neither is wrong. And the sooner we stop moralizing food, the sooner we can actually get curious about what we need.

You don't have to obey every craving, and you don't have to fight them, either. You can just *listen*. Ask, "What am I needing right now?" Sometimes the answer will be mashed potatoes. Sometimes it'll be a walk, a cry, or a nap. You are not a problem to fix — you are a person to nourish.

And speaking of that...

❦ Crisis Cravings Bingo

Here's a playful little way to track what your body (and heart) tends to want when the PMDD wave hits. Use this Bingo card as-is, or adapt it for your own cravings. The goal? To notice patterns, release shame, and maybe discover a few new go-to snacks that feel like a hug and a high five.

☐☐ Mark off what you crave when the chaos hits.

☐ Salty popcorn

☐ Melted cheese on literally anything

☐ Chocolate (duh)

☐ Warm soup or broth

☐ Carbs, carbs, carbs

☐ Something crunchy (rage chewing, but make it tasty)

☐ Peanut butter straight from the spoon

☐ Fruit (hello, grapes in the bathtub)

- ☐ Fizzy drink or soda
- ☐ A buttery baked good
- ☐ Just ice. Yes, chewing ice.
- ☐ Fast food, no regrets
- ☐ Spicy anything
- ☐ Cold and creamy (ice cream, yogurt, etc.)
- ☐ Something you ate as a kid

There's no prize for getting bingo, unless you count realizing you're not alone in your PMDD snack rituals. Because that's what this whole thing is really about: meeting yourself in the mess, with compassion and curiosity instead of judgment and shame.

The next time you find yourself staring into the fridge at midnight, holding back tears and wondering if it's okay to make nachos for dinner again, remember this: you're allowed. You're human. And food is not the enemy. Guilt is.

Eat what you need.

Love yourself anyway.

Repeat as necessary.

Chapter Nine

PMDD & Relationships:

Love & Conflict

Loving Me, Loving You:
PMDD in Romantic Relationships

PMDD doesn't ask for permission before barging into your love life. It doesn't politely knock. It kicks the door down, tracks mud across the carpet, and then demands to know why your partner didn't clean it up faster. Being in a romantic relationship while living with PMDD is like trying to do a three-legged race during an earthquake. There's stumbling, snapping, sometimes crying in the bathroom (or the hallway, or during brunch), and the occasional glorious moment where it all just... works.

There's this myth that once you find "your person," everything gets easier. That love, true love, should somehow shield you from your mental health challenges, that a good partner will fix the hard days, or that communication becomes effortless when you're with "the one." Let's gently but firmly call BS on that. Love does not make PMDD disappear. But it can make the ride less lonely, even beautiful in places, if both people know what they're up against.

The PMDD luteal phase can turn you into someone you barely recognize. Your partner might feel like they're walking on eggshells, or worse, feel like they've done something wrong when they haven't. One minute you're craving cuddles and affirmations; the next you're fantasizing about living alone in a lighthouse where nobody breathes too loudly. It's not about them. It's about the brain chemistry hijacking your body and mood and making you question everything, including whether love is even real or just a scam invented by people who never had to manage hormone hell.

Loving someone with PMDD takes patience, yes. But being the person with PMDD and still choosing to love? That takes courage. It's an act of bravery to open yourself up to intimacy when your emotions feel like a minefield. To say, "I'm not okay right now, but I still care about you. I still want to do this with you." That's powerful.

Of course, it's not always that poetic. Sometimes it's more like yelling "I'm sorry I said you breathe too loud, I just need 48 hours and some pasta and I'll love you again." And that's okay too.

A big part of navigating love with PMDD is learning how to communicate what you need, especially when what you need might change from one week to the next. You might need space, reassurance, help with dinner, or someone to just hold your hand while you cry and swear at the moon. Your partner won't always get it right, and that's normal. What matters is that they try, that you both keep showing up, and that forgiveness flows both ways. (And maybe that you have a shared calendar with "Luteal Alert!" stickers.)

There may be arguments that don't make sense in retrospect. Times when you overreact and know you're overreacting but can't stop it in the moment. That's not failure. That's biology behaving badly.

Having rituals of repair can be a relationship superpower: a shared language for "Hey, that was hard. Let's figure it out together."

Intimacy, too, can become a complicated dance. Some months you may feel connected, magnetic, even electric. Other months, the idea of being touched makes your skin crawl. PMDD isn't just mood swings, it can disrupt desire, shift how your body feels, and make vulnerability feel like too much. The key is honesty. Not just with your partner, but with yourself. Being able to say, "I love you, but right now I need to be in my own bubble," is an act of self-respect, not rejection. And the right partner? They'll learn that bubble-time doesn't mean love is gone. It just means the hormones are screaming louder than your heart can speak.

Building relationship literacy together, figuring out how PMDD shows up for *you*, and how your partner can support without overstepping, is an ongoing process. It's not about perfection. It's about teamwork. It's about tagging each other in and out, sharing the emotional load, and laughing at the absurdity of it all when you can. ("Remember when I cried because the kettle was too loud? Good times.")

PMDD will test your relationship, no question. But it also offers an unusual opportunity: the chance to build a love that's fiercely honest, tender in the hard times, and rooted in mutual growth. The kind of love that says, "I see all of you, including the parts that feel messy or unlovable, and I'm staying."

So, to those navigating love while being periodically unhinged: you're not broken, you're not too much, and you're not alone. You're just doing your best in a body that sometimes forgets how to be gentle. And that? That deserves a love as strong and soft and real as you are.

Reflection Questions

1. When I'm in the thick of PMDD, what kind of support do I *actually* need from a partner, and how can I communicate that more clearly when I'm feeling regulated?
2. What does a "safe love" look and feel like to me, and how can I protect that even when my hormones try to convince me otherwise?
3. How has PMDD shaped the way I see myself in relationships? Have I internalized any guilt or shame that isn't actually mine to carry?
4. What patterns or triggers tend to show up in my relationships during my luteal phase? What might I do differently (or ask for) to navigate them with more self-compassion?
5. In what ways has a partner shown up for me that felt truly supportive or grounding? How can I express appreciation or encourage more of that?
6. What boundaries do I need in place during my PMDD days to feel emotionally safe, and what makes it hard for me to maintain those boundaries?

7. How do I want to be loved on my hard days, and how do I want to love others when I'm feeling whole again?
8. Do I ever confuse PMDD-fuelled thoughts with relationship truths? How can I practice separating hormonal noise from my deeper knowing?
9. What myths about love, relationships, or emotional "stability" am I ready to let go of in order to build something more real and more me?

Breakups, Boundaries & The Blame Game

There's nothing quite like a breakup with PMDD in the mix. One minute you're sobbing into your pillow convinced no one will ever love you again, the next you're rage-cleaning your kitchen while muttering things like *"I hope they choke on their emotional unavailability."*

Breakups are already a chaotic, soul-cracking ride, but throw in premenstrual dysphoric disorder and suddenly you're navigating heartbreak while your hormones are also personally trying to end you.

PMDD most likely didn't ruin your relationship. A relationship that ends, whether slowly unravelled or violently exploded, ends because it wasn't right, or it wasn't sustainable, or you were tired of dimming your light to keep someone else comfortable. PMDD may have poured gasoline on the fire, sure. But the fire was already there.

People with PMDD are often misread. "Too intense." "Too needy." "So emotional." But here's the thing: sensitivity is not a flaw. Deep emotional range is not a red flag. If someone couldn't handle the real you, the hormonal, hurting, human you, they were never going to rise to the occasion of loving you fully. You deserve someone who doesn't flinch when you're raw, someone who stays soft when your world turns sharp.

And yet… the shame creeps in, doesn't it? The little voice whispering, *"Maybe it was you. Maybe you were too much."* Especially when you replay the luteal phase arguments, the misfired texts, the emotional landslides that left you exhausted and misunderstood. PMDD has this cruel way of making you doubt yourself, even when you know deep down that you were trying your damn best in a body that sometimes acts like it's running on glitchy software.

Let's name it: the guilt after a breakup can feel enormous. You might wonder if you scared them off. You might feel like you have to explain or defend yourself, like you owe them a PowerPoint presentation titled *"Why My Brain Chemistry Isn't a Personality Defect."* But you don't owe them anything. Not your shame. Not your silence. Not a sanitized version of your truth.

This is where boundaries come in, not just with them, but with yourself. Boundaries are not just about telling someone else "No." Sometimes, they're about telling yourself, *"I will not replay that argument for the 47th time today. I will not spiral into old stories that say I'm unlovable. I will not twist myself into emotional origami to make sense of their discomfort."*

PMDD can complicate breakups because it distorts your perception of everything, including your own worth. But here's the reframe: your sensitivity is a compass. Your deep emotions are not excess baggage, they're proof you felt it all. And that means you showed up. Fully, bravely, beautifully.

So yes, maybe you yelled. Maybe you shut down. Maybe you said things you didn't mean because your brain chemistry was throwing a tantrum. That doesn't make you toxic. That makes you someone navigating a condition that hijacks your nervous system and still showing up for love anyway. That is not a flaw. That's resilience.

After the dust settles, the most radical thing you can do is rewrite your story without them in it. Not as the villain or the hero, but just as someone who was never meant to carry you through the storm. You get to be the one who carries you now. You get to build a life that doesn't shrink to accommodate anyone else's fragility. You get to create boundaries that say, *"This is who I am. This is what I need. If that scares you, you're welcome to leave, but I will no longer abandon myself to be loved."*

It might be messy. It might be lonely sometimes. But it's also the beginning of something holy: a relationship with yourself that doesn't hinge on being "easy" or "low-maintenance" or "palatable." Because the truth is, if they couldn't handle you at luteal, they didn't deserve you at follicular. Period.

And now? You're free.

Chapter Ten

Parenting with PMDD

(a.k.a. Superhero Mode with a Side of Meltdown)

The Guilt Spiral

When You Love Them Fiercely but Still Lose Your Sh*t

There are days when you wake up with the best intentions: You're going to be present, patient, and emotionally available. You've packed the snack box with cucumbers carved into tiny stars, kissed little foreheads, and promised yourself that today, *today*, will be the day you keep it together.

And then, thirty-seven minutes later, someone spills an entire bottle of maple syrup on the dog, the toddler is screaming because the "wrong" socks are touching their ankles, and you feel something primal rising up in your chest. You snap. Maybe you yell. Maybe you slam a cupboard. Maybe you lock yourself in the bathroom and sob into a towel. Whatever form it takes, that tidal wave of PMDD-powered rage or despair crashes over your good intentions and leaves you gasping for air, clinging to the wreckage of your emotional bandwidth.

Welcome to the guilt spiral.

PMDD guilt isn't regular parenting guilt. It's guilt dipped in rage frosting, sprinkled with shame, and baked at the core of your identity. It hits differently when the explosion feels almost out-of-body, when you know it's your hormones hijacking the ship, but the fallout still lands squarely on your family. You love your kids with an intensity that could melt steel, and yet there are moments where just *being around them* feels like too much. The noise, the chaos, the clinginess—all of it becomes unbearable in a body that's already on fire.

Then comes the inner monologue:

"What kind of mother gets angry at their kid for asking for another snack?"
"I'm ruining them."
"I should be able to handle this."

It's brutal. And it's also incredibly human.

What's important to remember is that PMDD doesn't erase your love. Losing your temper doesn't cancel out the bedtime cuddles, the way you instinctively check they're breathing in the middle of the night, or how you'd throw yourself in front of a bus for them without blinking. The rage isn't the real you, it's the PMDD. It's your brain being chemically out of balance, not a moral failing.

Even when you know that, the guilt still comes. It sticks around long after the symptoms have passed, whispering that you're too much, or not enough, or somehow both. But guilt, while painful, can be a sign that you *care*. The trick is not letting it become your default setting.

Reframing the "bad days" is essential. Your child doesn't need a perfect parent, they need a *real* one. One who says, "I'm sorry I yelled earlier, I was having a hard time. It wasn't your fault." One who shows them how to come back from a mistake, how to take responsibility, and how to love themselves even when they're not at their best.

Repair is powerful. In fact, research shows that repairing after conflict, especially with kids, is more important than never messing up in the first place. Your child learns emotional resilience not from your flawless behaviour, but from watching you come back from the hard moments with honesty and love.

So, no, you're not the Pinterest mom. You're not folding fitted sheets with grace or turning recycled toilet rolls into STEM crafts during your luteal phase. But you are showing up. Even when your brain chemistry is working against you, even when you're stretched to the edge of what feels survivable, you're still here. Loving fiercely. Trying. Repairing. And that matters more than any picture-perfect version of parenthood ever could.

You're not a bad parent. You're a human mom with a hormonal landmine built into your cycle. And you're doing your best. On the good days, that looks like baking cupcakes together. On the hard days, it might look like surviving until bedtime with minimal emotional casualties. Either way, you are not alone, and you are not failing.

You are *fierce*.

You are *flawed*.

You are *forgiving*.

And even on your worst days, you are exactly the parent your child needs.

Battle Planning

Organizing Life Around the Hormonal Apocalypse

Living with PMDD means you don't get the luxury of just "winging it." While other people might plan their month around birthdays or school holidays, we're over here planning around an emotional category five hurricane that rolls in like clockwork every. single. month.

This chapter isn't about perfection. It's not about turning your life into a synchronized ballet of colour-coded charts and magical solutions. It's about *survival*. It's about finding ways to soften the blow, to make space for the chaos, and to get ahead of the meltdown instead of being steamrolled by it.

Because when you know the storm is coming, you can at least close the windows and hide the good snacks.

First things first: **cycle tracking is your new best friend**. Whether you use an app, a paper calendar, or a post-it note stuck to the fridge, the goal is to figure out when the monster weeks hit. Most people with PMDD have that lovely little premenstrual hell window that lasts anywhere from a few days to a couple of weeks. Once you know your pattern, you can start preparing like the hormonal doomsday prepper you were always meant to be.

You're not a robot. When your brain chemistry goes haywire, even brushing your teeth can feel like climbing Everest. So why on earth would you try to meal-plan, fold laundry, or answer 700 school emails during that time? You wouldn't, because you're smart. And tired. Very tired.

Enter: **freezer meals and mental load offloading.** Think of your follicular phase (the good one!) as your productivity sweet spot. That's when you do the things. Make the extra batch of soup. Write the to-do lists. Set up that "what to do if Mum is spiralling" chart for your partner or older kids. Trust me, future-you will sob with gratitude when there's something edible in the freezer and the house hasn't descended into feral chaos.

Then there's tag-team parenting. If you have a co-parent, *use them*. This is not the time for pride or quiet martyrdom. This is the time for texting your partner "I need you on full bedtime duty for the next 3 nights or I will physically melt into the carpet." If you're solo parenting, this is where **"prepping the village"** becomes essential. That might be a neighbour, a friend, a grandparent, a fellow PMDD warrior-mum who can swap "I'll take your kids for 2 hours today, you take mine next week" favours. You don't need a massive support team, just *one* reliable person who knows the drill can make a world of difference.

And then there's the part no one talks about: setting expectations with your kids. This doesn't mean trauma-dumping your symptoms onto a six-year-old, but it *does* mean using age-appropriate language to normalize that sometimes Mum has hard days. "I'm feeling overwhelmed right now, and it's not your fault." "I love you lots, I just need some quiet." These tiny scripts build emotional literacy *and* give you permission to be human. They won't always get it. Sometimes they'll scream in your face anyway. But you're planting seeds. And seeds grow.

Proactive planning isn't about eliminating PMDD, it's about giving yourself a fighting chance to get through it without collapsing. It's about accepting your limits, not as a weakness, but as a *strategy*. It's asking, "What can I do now to make things easier for future-me when she's hormonal, exhausted, and dangerously close to crying over mismatched socks?"

Realistically some months the plan will fall apart. The freezer will be empty, the tag team will bail, and you'll be eating dry cereal in a laundry pile while your kids reenact WWE. That's okay too. This isn't about winning. It's about surviving. You don't need to do it all. You need to do *enough* to get through.

So, build your battle plan. Even if it's duct tape and prayers. Because you're not weak, you're tactical. And that, my friend, is pure PMDD-powered badassery.

Help Is Not a Weakness

Learning to Delegate, Ask, and Receive

Asking for help does *not* mean you've failed. It doesn't mean you're lazy. It doesn't mean you're not trying hard enough. And it absolutely doesn't mean you've failed in any way, shape or form. It just means you're *human*, a human navigating life with a premenstrual disorder that occasionally makes even basic tasks feel like pushing a boulder uphill in roller skates.

But for some reason, so many of us treat "help" like it's a dirty word. We'd rather grin and bear it (okay, *rage-weep and bear it*) than say, "Hey, I'm drowning." Especially if we're the go-to, the organizer, the one who "has it all together." Spoiler: even the most capable people need support. Especially the most capable people.

The truth is, when PMDD is in full swing, your mental load becomes *Olympic-level*. There's the overwhelm, the sensory overload, the executive dysfunction, the irritability, the grief, the rage, the panic, and all while trying to parent, work, be a partner or a friend, and occasionally shower. The to-do list becomes this impossible mountain, and instead of climbing it, you lie under it and cry.

This is exactly when you need help the most. And yet, this is *also* when you're least likely to ask for it.

So let's practice something radical: **delegating**.

No, not because you're defeated. Because you're *smart*. You're protecting your limited energy for the things that actually matter. Letting someone else pick up milk, run the dishwasher, or take the kids to the park for 30 minutes isn't weakness. It's strategy. It's saying, "My needs matter too."

But what if help doesn't come automatically? That's when we move to step two: asking for it. Yes, it's uncomfortable. Yes, it can feel vulnerable or awkward. But you don't need a poetic TED Talk. You just need honesty. Try, "I'm in a rough patch with PMDD and I could use [X]. Can you help me out this week?" Or, "I need to step back for a minute so I don't lose my mind, can you take over for a bit?"

People often *want* to help. They just don't know what to do. Give them the manual. Make it easy. "Could you pick the kids up on Friday?" "Can you send me dinner ideas because my brain is jelly?" "Can I just vent to you for five minutes without fixing anything?"

Once you *get* help, you have to do the hardest thing of all, receive it without guilt.

You are allowed to rest. You are allowed to let someone else carry the load without immediately plotting how to repay them. You are allowed to sit down while someone else folds the damn towels, even if they don't fold them the "right" way (they *never* do, do they?). Let it go. Choose your sanity over symmetrical linen.

This is where the healing starts, not just in managing the symptoms, but in *believing* that your wellbeing is worthy of care. You're not meant to do this alone. PMDD is hard enough without martyring yourself on top of it.

So, build your support system. Big or small. Whether it's your partner, your best friend, your neighbour, your group chat, or that one mum from school who actually gets it. If you don't have anyone right now, know this: you still deserve help. You still deserve ease. And it *will* come. Keep asking. Keep reaching. You are not a burden, you're just a brilliant human who sometimes needs a hand.

📝 Scripts for Asking for Help (When Your Brain is on Fire)

Use them. Copy them. Mumble them through gritted teeth if you have to.

When you just need a break:
"I'm really struggling right now with PMDD. Could you take over for a bit so I can reset?"
"I need 20 minutes alone or I'm going to lose my mind—can you cover the kids?"
"Can you entertain them for half an hour so I can sit in silence and pretend I don't exist?"

When you need something practical done:

"Hey, can you grab a few things from the shop for me? I'm not in a good headspace to go out."

"I need help with dinner tonight—can you handle it or just order something?"

"The washing situation is getting apocalyptic. Could you please run a load?"

When you're emotionally flooded and need to talk:

"I don't need a solution, I just need to vent. Can you listen for five minutes?"

"I'm feeling really low and overwhelmed today. Can I check in with you later if it gets worse?"

"I'm spiralling a bit. Can you remind me that this will pass?"

When you're prepping your village ahead of the storm:

"Next week is my PMDD window—can I book in some support now so I'm not scrambling?"

"Just a heads-up, I'll probably need some extra help during my rough days next week."

"Would you be open to doing a little swap—like you take the kids one afternoon and I'll return the favour later?"

You don't need to sound perfect. You don't need to justify your ask with a 12-slide PowerPoint presentation. You just need to start. Speak up in whatever way feels doable, and if words fail you, send this page to your person and circle what you need.

Because you're allowed to ask. You're allowed to receive. You deserve support, not when you've hit rock bottom, but always.

Chapter Eleven

You Are Not Your PMDD:

Finding Joy, Identity, and Power Again

Reclaiming Me:

Who I Am Beyond the Storm

There's a quiet, aching grief that comes with PMDD, one that rarely gets acknowledged. It's not just the mood swings or the exhaustion or the way you feel hijacked by your own hormones, it's the slow, creeping fear that you've lost yourself in it all. That somewhere between the anger, the sadness, and the spirals, you disappeared.

I remember staring in the mirror one day and thinking, "Where did I go?" I wasn't sure who the person looking back at me was anymore. She was tired, sharp-edged, and surviving. And I missed the version of me who used to laugh easily, who made spontaneous plans, who could sit in her own mind without feeling like it was on fire.

This chapter is for that version of you.

The one you think you lost.

PMDD can make your world feel smaller, but it doesn't erase who you are. You're still in there. Maybe not as loud, maybe tucked behind a fortress of coping mechanisms and survival mode, but not gone.

Rediscovering yourself doesn't require some dramatic life overhaul. It's not about quitting your job to live in a cabin or finding the perfect self-care routine (although, no shame if that's your vibe). It's in the quiet things. The rituals that remind you of who you are when PMDD isn't steering the wheel.

For me, it started with playlists. I made one for the version of myself I missed, songs that made me feel vibrant, connected, capable. Then came journaling, not the serious kind, just scribbles and swears and "ugh"s. Somewhere in there, I started wearing red lipstick again. It wasn't about looking good, it was about feeling a little more *me*, even on the days my brain was trying to convince me I was too much or not enough.

I began choosing things on purpose, little identity breadcrumbs that said, "Hey, I remember you." A favourite hoodie that felt like a hug. A boundary that whispered, "You're allowed to say no." A spontaneous solo coffee date because I actually like my own company when I'm not in crisis.

It's also about learning to separate *you* from the *symptoms*. PMDD might make you feel angry, anxious, or hopeless, but that doesn't mean you *are* those things. You are not your rage. You are not your panic. You are not your darkest thought during luteal limbo. You're the one who survives them. You're the one who comes back every single month, scarred maybe, but still standing.

It's messy. Some months you'll feel powerful and aligned and other months you'll eat cereal for dinner and cry because you dropped your keys. That's not failure. That's living with something hard and doing your damn best.

If I could go back and tell my younger self something, it would be this: you're allowed to take up space, even when you're not at your best. You don't have to wait until you're symptom-free to start reclaiming joy or rebuilding yourself. Start now, as you are, stormy and soft and everything in between.

You are not gone. You are still here, waiting to be found in the smallest of moments, the right song, the laugh you didn't expect, the quiet strength you show just by getting through another cycle.

And piece by piece, you'll remember her.

You'll remember *you*.

Joy Isn't Cancelled:
Making Space for Light in Dark Cycles

There's a strange kind of guilt that can show up when you find yourself smiling during a PMDD week. Like you're somehow cheating the system. Like you're not allowed to feel good because the calendar says your hormones are supposed to be dragging you into the trenches. Here's the truth: joy isn't cancelled just because PMDD is in session.

This chapter is your permission slip to feel good, yes, even during the hard days. Especially during the hard days.

I used to think I had to wait. Wait until I felt stable, level, "normal" (whatever that means). Like joy was a destination only accessible when all the mental health stars aligned. But waiting for a symptom-free day can sometimes feel like waiting for a unicorn to show up with a latte and a winning lottery ticket. So I stopped waiting.

That shift didn't come with fireworks or grand gestures. It came with little rebellions. The kind of tiny, defiant acts that say, "I still get to live." I started lighting a candle I loved, even if my brain felt like a horror movie. I bought a houseplant just to watch something thrive. I made pancakes for dinner because, frankly, pancakes are joy on a plate.

These weren't cures. They didn't erase the pain or stop the spirals. But they gave me something else to hold onto. A flicker of light in the hormonal storm. And those flickers matter. They're not frivolous. They're resistance.

PMDD wants to convince you that everything is bleak. That you're too much, or not enough, or doomed to feel like this forever. And joy is the middle finger to all of that. It doesn't mean you're ignoring the pain, it means you're choosing to believe that pain isn't the only thing you get to feel.

Sometimes, the joy looks ridiculous. Dancing like a weirdo to a trashy pop song while crying? Joy. Watching a comfort show you've seen 43 times and quoting every line? Joy. Laughing at a meme when five minutes ago you were convinced life was a void? Still joy.

And here's the thing: you don't have to earn it. You don't need to finish your to-do list or "snap out of it" or be in the follicular phase to deserve a good moment. Joy isn't a reward for functioning. It's a birthright. One that still belongs to you even when everything feels hard.

What I wish I knew sooner is that feeling good isn't betrayal. It's healing. You're allowed to have good days inside bad weeks. You're allowed to laugh even if you cried this morning. You're allowed to want more than just surviving.

The goal isn't constant happiness. That's exhausting and unrealistic and honestly kind of boring. The goal is room. Room for laughter and softness and pleasure to exist alongside the hard. To make space for joy to sneak in through the cracks, even if it only stays for a minute.

So, here's to joy that doesn't wait for permission. Joy that shows up unshowered, unmedicated, a little chaotic. Joy that's soft and stubborn and yours.

Even in the middle of the mess, you still get to live. You still get to feel good. You still get to laugh. Joy isn't cancelled. Not now. Not ever.

Stronger Together:

The Power of PMDD Sisterhood

There's a particular kind of loneliness that comes with PMDD. A silent kind. You can be surrounded by people who love you and still feel like you're screaming into a void that no one else hears. Because how do you explain that your brain turns against you once a month? That some days, brushing your teeth feels like climbing a mountain, or that you're afraid of your own thoughts even when nothing is technically "wrong"?

For a long time, I thought it was just me.

That's the magic of community. That moment when someone else says, *"Same."* Not "that sucks," or "have you tried yoga?" or "you're just hormonal," but *"Me too. I've been there. You're not crazy. I get it."* It's like air after holding your breath for years.

Finding your PMDD people changes things. It doesn't erase the struggle, but it makes the weight a little lighter. Suddenly, you're not carrying it alone. There are others out there who know exactly what it feels like to count the days, to dread the luteal shift, to apologize for things you don't remember doing or saying. And they don't just understand, they validate you without question.

The best part? You don't need a massive support circle. One person can be enough. One friend, one online group, one voice in the dark saying, *"Hey, I'm here too."* You can find these connections in PMDD Facebook groups, forums, subreddits, Instagram DMs, even in the comment section of a meme post that hits way too close to home. These are real connections. They count.

And if you can't find your people right away, it's okay to *build* the space you need. Talk about it, post about it, wear your PMDD awareness hoodie to the pharmacy, whatever feels right. Sharing your story isn't an obligation. You don't owe anyone your pain. But when you do choose to share, something powerful happens. You become the mirror for someone else. You become the "same" they've been searching for.

What I wish I knew earlier is this: you were never alone. Not even when it felt like it. Not in the worst, darkest, ugliest moments. There's an entire community out there with battle scars and soft hearts, ready to sit in the storm with you without asking you to explain yourself.

The PMDD sisterhood is real. It's fierce. It's funny as hell. It's full of rage and empathy and resilience and late-night check-ins. It's a place where you can say, "I feel like a monster today," and someone replies, "Same, want to talk or scream into the void together?"

And that, *that*, is healing.

So, if you're still searching, don't give up. Your people are out there. They're making memes, starting group chats, mailing each other hormone tea and heating pads. They're proof that solidarity doesn't have to be loud to be life-changing. Sometimes, it's just a message that says, "You got this." Or, "I've got you."

You were never meant to carry this alone.

And now, you don't have to.

Still Here, Still You

So here we are. You've made it to the end of this book, and if that feels like an accomplishment, it absolutely is. Because chances are, you've read it through brain fog, cramps, mood crashes, maybe even through tears or numbness or pure exhaustion. Or maybe you devoured it on one of the good days, when the sky felt clear again. Either way, you showed up. And that matters.

Living with PMDD is not just a health condition. It's a constant negotiation between who you know yourself to be and who your hormones sometimes try to convince you you are. It's a cycle of remembering and forgetting, losing yourself and finding pieces again, falling apart and rebuilding. Over and over. It's brutal. It's beautiful. It's unfair. And it's real.

There's no shiny bow to tie on top of this journey. I won't pretend there's a cure-all hiding in the next paragraph. But there *is* something even better: the reminder that you are not alone and you are not powerless. Not every chapter in your life will be written in crisis mode. There will be joy, connection, and peace, sometimes in unexpected places.

By now, you've met parts of yourself you maybe hadn't named before: the tender one, the fierce one, the one who keeps going even when she swears she can't. You've read stories that sound a little too familiar, cried at lines that hit too hard, maybe even laughed at the chaos of it all. That's what healing sometimes looks like. Not a straight line. More like a tangled necklace you slowly, patiently work to unknot.

I want to leave you with this: PMDD may be part of your life, but it is not the whole of it. You are still allowed to dream big, to love loudly, to rest deeply, to laugh like a lunatic at inappropriate memes, to say "no," to say "help," and to say "this is who I am now, and I'm still figuring it out."

You're allowed to be a walking contradiction, tired and strong, struggling and hopeful, fed up and still fighting. You're allowed to change your mind. You're allowed to have bad days. And you're allowed, always, to take up space.

If this book has done one thing, I hope it's reminded you of your softness and your strength. Of how valid your experience is. Of how brave it is to live inside a body and brain that doesn't always play nice, and still find ways to be kind to yourself anyway.

You're still here. Still fighting. Still *you*.

And that's more than enough.

♥ Thank You

To you, the reader, thank you for picking up this book and spending time with it.

Living with PMDD can be overwhelming, isolating, and misunderstood, but I hope these pages offered you a little clarity, comfort, or connection.

Whether you're just starting to understand PMDD or have been managing it for years, I'm grateful to have shared this space with you.

You're strong, you're not alone, and you deserve support every step of the way.

"I am allowed to rest. I am allowed to be kind to myself. I am allowed to take up space, even when PMDD tells me otherwise."

Printed in Dunstable, United Kingdom